NEAREST THE SUN

NEAREST THE SUN
The Story of Project Dengke

Mel Richardson

Eagle

Trowbridge

Terra Nova Publications

© Mel Richardson 2002

First published by Eagle Publishing Ltd, 2002
Terra Nova Publications Ltd, 2002

Published in Great Britain by
Eagle Publishing Ltd
6 Kestrel House, Mill Street, Trowbridge, Wiltshire BA14 8BE
and
Terra Nova Publications Ltd
PO Box 2400, Bradford on Avon, Wiltshire BA15 2YN

ISBN   0 86347 569 8   [Eagle]

ISBN   1 90194 920 6   [Terra Nova]

Printed in Wales by CPD, Ebbw Vale

Contents

Acknowledgements

I dedicate this book, freely acknowledge and thank the myriad of people who have made it possible. Firstly, there are the team members, supporters and sponsors who are listed in the Appendices and others who are mentioned in the text. Secondly, all those individuals who have given so generously in money and prayer. Thirdly, the *Care and Share Foundation* Honorary Patrons and Trustees. Fourthly, those who have given very kind and generous endorsements, including: Fiona Castle; Sir Ranulph Fiennes Bt OBE; Sir Cliff Richard OBE; Sir Denis Rooke OM CBE FRS FREng; and Squadron Leader Mike Cole OBE. Finally, most importantly of all, my family and my extended family, very especially Jackie, and Matthew, Mark, Angela, Rachel, Riley, Evan, Lily, Michael, David, and my brothers Keith and Brian; and, of course, Mum and Dad. Thank you so much!

FOREWORD

Fiona Castle

I have been very challenged by reading *Nearest the Sun*. It is easy for people, including Christians, to become aware of disasters and injustices in the world and then decide that the problems are so overwhelming that there is nothing they can do about them. Well, this is a book to prise us out of our comfort zones, and to prove that while we cannot change the world there is always something we can do to lessen the suffering of other people. I have long been aware of the intrepid nature of Mel Richardson —a man of vision, who inspires others to 'boldly go where no man has gone before'. This story of his demonstrates this. From sponsors, donors and the retired, through to the highly qualified professionals, God provides the teams to bring his vision into reality: wonderful evidence of the Body of Christ working together, each part needing all the others.

Many of the pages you will read are filled with heart-stopping excitement and suspense —and it is all TRUE! It has been said that 'courage is fear that has said its prayers'. I am sure you will agree that this story must have contained many such prayers, and as such is a salutary lesson to us all. May God bless all those who had the courage to say yes to him.

God bless you, Mel. I am in awe of the things you have done, and what you have achieved.

PROLOGUE

Squadron Leader Michael Cole OBE

The wild beauty and breathtaking scenery of south west China, together with the headwaters of the mighty Yangtze, have been an unrealised challenge to expeditions for several centuries. In 1990, using hovercraft, a British expedition labelled 'an adventure with a (humanitarian) purpose' sought to reach the source of the great river whilst engaging in medical and solar energy projects to support isolated peoples. Overcoming many obstacles, and after years of patient waiting, the expedition was rewarded by the depth of friendship received from the ordinary Chinese and Tibetan people. A valuable but fragile bridge had been built. The ultimate success of the 1990 expedition was not only in the short term advance, a unique journey to the river's source, or the project goals realised, but in the subsequent long term commitment to the area by Dr Mel Richardson. His sense of purpose and perseverance, over twelve years in building on this early advance, has been remarkable.

The success of Mel and his teams in achieving so much for the people of Dengke has reached far beyond the local area, and has made an important contribution to Sino-British friendship.

INTRODUCTION

Sir Denis Rooke OM, CBE, FRS, FREng.

I first knew Dr Mel Richardson when he was a Senior Lecturer in Materials Engineering at Loughborough University, of which I am Chancellor.   One day, he told me of his involvement in the forthcoming British Hovercraft Expedition to seek the source of the Yangtze. That expedition was brilliantly successful in technical terms and delivered some humanitarian benefits also, but more importantly opened the eyes of Richardson to the difficult lifestyle of the peoples of the remote, rugged and inhospitable Tibetan Plateau. Despite the rigours of their daily lives, he found the people warm and friendly, and felt impelled to do his best to ameliorate their lot.

Through the excellent relations established on that Hovercraft Expedition, he received official invitations to return at any time to this normally 'closed area'. He set up the charitable *Care and Share Foundation* and through that has planned and led three further humanitarian expeditions to the region. These have been centred on a village called Dengke, which sits alongside the Yangtze at a height of some 11,500 feet in the Tibetan Autonomous Prefecture and had been the site of the first hovercraft base.

This book is a partial record of the series of adventures of the volunteers inspired by the author, and is the precursor to a further, more ambitious project to fund an International Friendship Centre at Dengke, to build on the success of the numerous collaborative projects in being, and establish a permanent resource centre to provide long term support to the peoples of the region.

The imagination, organising ability, dedication and sheer energy of Dr Richardson has already brought mighty humanitarian benefits, but in my view this further project deserves the enthusiastic support of all readers of the book.

PART ONE

Essence of Adventure

Professor Mel Richardson MBE

Chapter One

On The Edge of Danger

The gun was raised. The intention was clear. The soldier had orders to shoot anyone taking pictures of bridges. We had innocently stopped for a few minutes by the side of the river. A few people with telephoto lenses were taking pictures of a flimsy old bamboo bridge, next to the main concrete structure across which we had just passed. It was all quite harmless: members of the group were just snapping away. Someone had the presence of mind to throw himself quickly on the guy, smothering the gun and moving his arm in another direction. Providentially, no one was hurt on that occasion. Our army permit had been quite clear, indicating that we were allowed into this closed area, providing no pictures of bridges were taken. We had forgotten that restriction.

That was just one adventure amongst many on the British Hovercraft Expedition to China. We had come through landslides. We had experienced horrendous ice and snow, and lorries sliding across the side of mountain faces. We had survived crashes and smash-ups on rocks in huge rapids on the Yangtze River. We had battled through some incredible conditions and amazing situations with local officials. That was back in 1990, during what was to be the forerunner to an even more breathtaking series of adventures which we have called 'Project Dengke', in an area graphically described as "nearest the sun" by a local Tibetan friend, Ang Luo.

Intrigued, people often ask, 'How did it all begin?' —A fair question, and one which is very easy to answer. In 1984, following a talk on his then latest expedition, Squadron Leader Mike Cole OBE wrote in my visitors' book: "Yangtze next stop. We need a plastics expert."

He had come to take a meeting at my local church, to share his adventures using hovercraft in the developing world, and to speak of the way he had expressed his Christian faith in practical ways by helping those in need. He challenged me, saying, "How about you? You're a Christian. Have you ever thought about using your skills and background to help others in difficult situations?" I must admit I had never really done so, nor even seriously thought about the matter. I had always dismissed this as being the sort of thing other people did. He continued, "Maybe you could use your unique sphere of influence in a practical way, and get some equipment to help people, through the special group of contacts that only you have. This could lead to an 'adventure with a purpose' for the future." My interest was aroused!

Several days after Mike Cole left, I and my wife, Jackie, found the words of challenge in the visitors' book. Initially, I thought he just wanted someone to be a consultant on materials for hovercraft, because at the time I was Senior Lecturer in Materials at the University of Loughborough. Progressively, I was drawn into the project as a whole, with its focus on the Far East. That was back in 1984. I had no idea it would take a further six years to reach the point when we would actually arrive in China and Tibet, and I would be tipped headlong into a tremendous adventure.

Following the success of the hovercraft expedition to China, my eyes were opened, with Rob Watson, John Whatmore and others, to the needs of the developing world. The world record-breaking project in 1990 highlighted for me the potential of 'adventures with a purpose', where Christians could build bridges for the gospel by using their God-given skills to influence and help those in need.

Knots, string and promises fulfilled

Dengke was the site of the first riverside base we established when en route, by hovercraft, to the source of the Yangtze River. Prior to this, in 1987, whilst poring over a German map as we planned a 'reccie' in China, we had decided to divide the first thousand miles of the river into equal stretches, where fuel dumps could be laid down. Thus it just 'happened' that the village of Dengke, later to become so close to my heart, lined up alongside the first of several equally spaced knots on a length of string. These were conveniently laid out like a snake along the winding path of the river on the map. So you could say I was 'led' into this village by the strangest of circumstances.

Whilst camping just outside this same village in 1990, I was deeply moved when an old goat-herd gave me one of his only possessions — a sling-shot made of goat and yak hair. Likewise, a young urchin girl named Udren gave up her only toy, a beat-up rubber ball, for Rob Watson, one of our pilots, to give to his daughter and the 'children of England'. I was touched by such sincere generosity, and felt prompted to promise members of the village, both old and young, that one day I would return to help them. Thus, in setting up a new charity called the 'Care and Share Foundation', and leading and planning Project Dengke 92, 95, 99, and so on, I was keeping my promise.

This fulfilled vow has since brought great joy into my life, as well as the pleasure of encouraging a whole new generation of dedicated young Christians from all over the world, to discover new 'adventures with a purpose'. With my wife, it has also been my pleasure to support and enable a young Chinese girl, Lily, (Chinese name Dai Ao-Li), and Ang Luo, a Tibetan born in Dengke, to come and study in England, and then to return home. Lily, in particular, has become very much a part of our family, and as our 'Chinese daughter' even now appears on our Christmas cards, along with her new husband. In 1997 I gave Lily away at her wedding in Chengdu, so now we have gained a Chinese son-in-law as well. More about them later.

New challenges

A world record certificate, given to us by the *Guinness Book of Records*, reads: *Dr Mel Richardson and nine crew in the hovercraft* Neste Enterprise *navigated the Yangtze River at a height of 4,983 metres, or 16,050 feet, on 11th June 1990.*

It was an awe-inspiring experience to be in such a remote location, almost totally cut-off (coincidentally, on the eighteenth birthday of my eldest son, Matthew). On the way to that record-breaking rendezvous, we had passed through the village of Dengke, a thousand miles from the source of the Yangtze. Dengke (sometimes spelt Dainkog), is in Sichuan Province, China. To give an idea of its size: if it were a country, it would be the eighth largest in the world. In the far west of the province is the Tibetan Autonomous Prefecture, Ganzi, and in the west of Ganzi is the tiny Tibetan Khamba-speaking area in which the town is situated. Dengke nestles alongside the Yangtze River. There is a bridge across, and on the other side is Tibetan Autonomous Region (TAR, as it is sometimes called). To the east, the Sichuan Province side of the river, is TAP (Tibetan Autonomous Prefecture).

It took two years, from 1990 to 1992, to assemble the volunteers, from all walks of life, to come with me to the tiny village. There were many hiccups on the way, and a multitude of problems. For example, the agent who was supplying our tickets to fly us out from the UK to China went bankrupt, and right up until the very last moment in 1992, we did not know whether we were going to get to where we wanted to go. Remarkably, *Alitalia* came through at the last minute, having learnt of the project that we had put together, and were very impressed that we wanted to go and help needy people in such a remote village. With great generosity, they supplied us with a complete set of tickets, free of charge, to replace the ones we had lost through the demise of the travel agent. So we flew out, praising the Lord, a team very much looking forward to an exciting adventure.

We intended to carry out a large range of activities on the expedition. The projects we had planned included scientific and engineering work. We were also to carry out school and hospital painting, and ICI had supplied £7,000-worth of paint for us to use for that purpose. We had school and hospital solar pump trials lined up. Some activities were spin-offs of projects that I had set up at Loughborough University. We had prototype solar water purifiers that we had been working on with my colleague Colin Garner in the Mechanical Engineering Department. We would be running field trials of prototype solar cookers. New materials were going to be exposed to the Tibetan environment, and there were several civil engineering construction evaluation projects. We had a medical team who were going to get involved in a cultural and technical exchange with the local doctors to see what could be done in the future, and we had an education team with some teachers, to see what could be done to develop the friendship that we had first created in 1990. We also planned some horseback excursions, and cultural exchanges with the local school.

All the team were volunteers. They were born-again Christians with a desire to help others, and to use whatever practical skills they had, to help those in need. Some came highly qualified, like the doctors; some came with muscle, and the ability to dig trenches. Others came with a skill to encourage others and make cups of tea, and maybe fill in some paperwork. Whether people were highly professional, or whether they came with no apparent skill at all, everyone could be used. Each person had a reason for being there, and a gift that could be used for God's glory.

Learning Lessons

One of our first problems, when our equipment arrived in Chengdu after a long tortuous journey across the world, was to find that it had been tampered with and broken into. This was a real worry, and it brought about some heartache and soul-searching. You see, amongst the kit that I had thought had been stolen or damaged was the particular jacket and trousers I had worn on the historic journey to the source of the Yangtze River. It was one of those possessions that you prize because it brings back such wonderful memories. For me, that particular equipment was very, very special. I thought I had lost it completely. I know it sounds strange, but I was extremely upset. But, it is amazing how God gets you to pray about these things. Although it meant nothing to other people, it meant a lot to me, and I prayed that I could come to the point where I could 'let go' of these material things and not be so distressed. After all, as they say, 'you cannot take it with you when you go'. What good are prized kit and jackets in heaven? The Lord helped me to see this, and to come to terms with it and say, "OK I let it go. Why am I getting so upset when there are so many more important issues?" At the moment of 'release' I felt strangely comfortable about the issue, and quite relaxed. In fact, I sensed that I was being taught a lesson about possessions. Imagine my surprise when, having come to terms with all this, the missing items re-appeared in the back of the container that had been broken into. A bit dirty, a bit mucked up, but there they were. My prized possessions were still there. It was almost as if the Lord had taken them away, taught me a lesson, and then given them back again!

The eight hundred mile journey from the capital of Sichuan Province, Chengdu through to Dengke is a long and dangerous one. We have to travel along precipitous mountain ledges and long, winding mountain roads. Sometimes they fall away; sometimes, huge rocks come down across the road, scattering all before them. Sometimes, vehicles end up at the bottom of chasms. Indeed, as we passed along one particular valley we saw a vehicle that had fallen down the side in a complete, crumpled mess at the bottom. When we investigated, we found villagers shouting at various people and we learnt that two drivers had been going along this narrow road, and had been racing each other, or trying to overtake for some reason. One had nudged the other over the edge, probably not deliberately, but just driving dangerously. Not surprisingly, the villagers were shouting; and there were people from the army, swinging rifle butts. There was a lot of commotion going on, which we had to pass through. I felt sick in my stomach to see bloody faces, and rough justice being meted out. Intervention proved impossible. This was just one of the many incidents that can occur on remote mountain roads.

On one journey, en-route to Kangding, we passed along not only these very dangerous elevated tracks, but also alongside some of the most beautiful scenery in the world. I remember especially Green Dragon Lake, serenely peaceful, amazingly beautiful, and free from all the usual encumbrances that one finds in tourist areas. Thankfully, the 'wrong sort' of tourists have not come to this region in any significant numbers as it is a 'closed' region. For a brief moment we sat and marvelled at the beauty of God's creation.

We also stopped and then traversed a chain bridge in the town of Luding. This is a very notable historic site where, during the Long March in the 1930s, the Communists moved across China to battle with the Nationalists, who were led by Chiang Kai Chek. On this very bridge a violent battle took place, which the Communists ultimately won. There is a saying in China that, 'He who takes Luding Bridge, takes China', and so it proved, as the Communists swept to power in the following years.

When we arrived in Kangding, which is the capital of Ganzi Prefecture, a big surprise awaited us. As we turned a corner, we were greeted by a great cacophony of sound as trumpets played, and young children dressed in traditional clothes lined up and waved and sang to us. It was a truly amazing welcome. In the town, a big party had been laid on for us, and we enjoyed the singing and the dancing, and the wonderful display of Tibetan culture that was spread before us. When

18

they asked us if we would 'do something', we stood up and sang the Kangding Love Song (the words of which are in Appendix D), and a recording of the song is available from our website (Appendix H). It is a very famous song, and they seemed to appreciate that we had taken the trouble to learn one of their best known folk tunes.

We continued our journey, and some miles outside of Dengke, several days later, we were amazed to find that a beautiful tent had been erected at the side of the road, where we were invited in to meet the local leaders. And then, as we continued our journey, maybe thirty or forty miles from Dengke, we suddenly became aware that hundreds of Tibetans in their traditional clothes were lining the route, giving us a really incredible welcome. Some of the people had been standing in the sun for many, many hours and this did not seem to have put them off at all. I said to the team, "If they've taken the trouble to wait for us, even though we've been delayed by landslides and other problems on the road, we must at least, take the trouble to meet and greet them, particularly the ordinary local people."

So I got the team out, and every time we came to a group of people who had been waiting specifically for us, we walked, instead of travelling in the bus. This was a great opportunity to wave and to shake hands, and say 'thank you' to them.

Alongside us, the warriors from the village were travelling by horseback, shouting, whooping and waving swords. All sorts of sounds were coming out of buildings alongside the road, as people played huge horns in welcome. When we finally arrived at Dengke itself, the welcome was even more overwhelming. The whole village turned out to greet us. They were singing and throwing hats in the air; they wanted to give us a wonderful welcome home, so to speak, having remembered that we had gone through the village two years before. It was very, very moving.

We finally took the truck into the compound, where a building had been set aside for our stay. It was a rather old, basic place with a straw bed for each member of the team.

Chapter Two

Goodbye Comfort

Loos and rumours of loos

One of the things that has become something of a folk legend amongst people who have come on Project Dengke expeditions is the state of the loos. In fact, they are nothing like the toilets we would expect in the West, or in a major Chinese city. Usually, in this part of the world, you do well if you get two planks across a very big pit, with an enormous pig sniffing around underneath you. It is something of a culture shock to be in a long line crouched over these holes in the floor. You may be blessed with a partition between you, but there would certainly be nothing in front. So you wander down the line of 'traps', passing various semi-naked people smoking, chatting to the next person, or maybe even reading a newspaper. It is amazing what one can get used to when nature calls!

On one occasion, one of our doctors, crouching on the famous 'Dengke loo', dropped his wallet into the immense cesspit. Imaginary bets were then taken as to how much had to be in a doctor's wallet in order for him to go down and get it out. The answer is—not very much! In fact, that particular doctor managed to get a piece of wire, which looked like a bent hanger, to extend and poke down the hole, and eventually hook the offending wallet out. On another occasion, someone's washing tackle went the same way and was retrieved by the same technique.

Doctor Gareth Clegg was so inspired by the Dengke loos that he wrote a 12-bar blues on his guitar and a group of team members sang it to us during one of the evening amusement sessions that we arranged to while away the time. The 'joint' swung to the sound *of The Dengke Loo Blues* and other dubious artistic compositions which, for those with a strong stomach, can be sampled in Appendix B.

Some of these 'way-out' loos are perched in the most extraordinary locations. One loo I recall, en-route to Dengke, was on the slopes of the 7500m high Mount Gongga, situated in a low-level glacier park which had some hot springs attached to it, where you could swim in the open air. The loo to the side had obviously been part of a landslip. So as you inched your way inside the wooden structure, and peered down the hole, instead of a pit, you saw an enormous precipice disappearing to the depths below you.

In 1999, the group who went up the mountains from Dengke to a village called Bengda found themselves using a loo in similar circumstances. It was perched across a precipice overlooking an area where, apparently, there were lots of wild birds and extraordinary rare animal life. Rumour has it that Paul Lund, one of our photographers, would crouch and spend hours overlooking this area, taking pictures of whatever came by. Like many places in China and Tibet, buildings often have a dual purpose. In this case the loo doubled as a bird hide.

Team members on a Project Dengke Expedition need a sense of humour. This is as true when en-route as when located in one particular place. The bottom line is you either laugh or you cry! Anyone who comes on one of my expeditions expecting a glamorous lifestyle quickly has their aspirations dispelled when we announce on the coach (miles from nowhere) that we are making a 'Special Presentation'. Everybody at some stage gets the famous 'runs', resulting in a desperate shout of 'Stop the Coach! Stop the Coach!' At this point a big cheer goes up, we stop the coach, and the victim dashes into the distance. On their return, just for a joke, we conduct an awards ceremony and make an appropriate presentation.

On the first occasion most of us visited Dengke, in 1990, we were part of the hovercraft expedition team, and actually dug our own latrine pits. These were great holes in the ground next to the Yangtze, and were no deeeper than about six feet. We put our own planks across. Rumour has it that Mike Cole had to rush to be the first desperate user.

Rumour also has it that he fell through. Someone was heard to comment, "It is good that he was not the second person testing it!"

Landslides, earthquakes and things that go bump in the night.
There are many hazards associated with journeys in this part of Western Sichuan and Tibet. Perennial problems are landslides, rock falls and earthquakes. These are extremely dangerous and very scary when you are caught in them. At times we have been driving along, either in a jeep, or in an old, beat-up coach, to find that the ground beneath us is moving sideways, potentially sliding us down the mountainside into an enormous canyon. Needless to say, this is terrifying!

At times like this, it tests your faith right to the very roots; a time, indeed, to turn to the Lord, and cry out for help, as many have done. When you are going along and you come to a huge block in the road, where you see huge boulders, larger than bungalows strewn across in front of you, and you can see the loose stones still in motion, believe me, it concentrates the mind. It makes one realise how great one's Almighty Protector really is.

On one occasion I remember, the coach was winding its way down a hill. People were getting extremely agitated, scared and worked up. Some were quiet, some were vocal, at which point I said, "OK, we claim to have faith, let's put it to the test." We got the song books out and I got the guitarists to play, even though we were bouncing all over the road. We started singing *How Great Thou Art* and other songs. It is wonderful how, when you turn to the Lord, he is always ready to answer, certainly in times of weakness, and in those times when we really need him.

The danger associated with mountain roads is no more aptly illustrated than in the 'rescue' story described later in this book, in Sandra Watson's Diary. Later, this story of our saving the lives of three Tibetans, who had fallen many hundreds of metres down a cliff, was featured in a *Readers Digest* article (selling worldwide 28 million copies in 17 languages) and more recently in their book of international rescues. When BBC TV made their '999 International Special Documentary' to recreate the adventure, I found it both fun and weird to have someone play my part. I joked to the producer, "Who is going to be cast in my role? Mel Gibson?" Quick as a flash, he joked back, "No, Mel Smith!" At least I think he was joking! What was extremely funny about the final programme was how my actor wandered about the cliff top (with considerable artistic licence), banging his head with his hands (something I have never ever done) trying to create the concept of leader wrestling with difficult decisions, how can we get to the injured, etc. The day after the showing, you can imagine the leg pulling in the coffee room at work. Also hilarious was that one of the rescuers (Niels Kofoed —affectionately known as the Great Dane from Denmark) was given a strong cockney accent i.e. "all wight, mate" and all that stuff!

Round about 1992 or 1993, that sort of time, I remember I was giving a talk about a previous Project Dengke adventure in Melton Mowbray Baptist Church. A lady came up to me, Vera Pooley, a retired midwife, and said, "When I was younger I would have loved to come on one of your expeditions."

I said to her, "Well, what's the problem? Age is not a barrier these days. Is your heart in the right place? Do you have the desire, do you indeed have the calling to want to come with us? Whether you're re-tired or not, everybody has some skill which can be used for the Lord, whether it be practical service, or highly professional skill, or maybe a particular spiritual gift which can be shared with others, to encourage and to strengthen."

I remember some time later, after Vera had accepted the invitation to come with us, we were travelling along a mountain road when, again, we encountered enormous rockfalls. There seemed to have been some sort of landslide: the result of an earthquake, perhaps. We were inch-ing along the road, alongside a sheer drop of many hundred metres, with no protection. The wheels were hanging over the edge of the cliff! Vera turned from the front of the coach and shouted down to me, "When you told me it was this dangerous, I didn't really believe you. I thought it was artistic licence, but now I can see what you mean." Her words combined jesting and fearfulness.

I said something like, "Vera, just pray. Just trust. And even bet-ter, just slide down in your seat and go to sleep—and whatever you do, don't look out of the window." Over the years, I have found this to be very good advice: Trust in the Lord, pray; rely on his strength. Look up to the hills and apply the teaching of the psalmist, saying: That is where my strength comes from. Then slide down in your seat and try to get some sleep. At least, close your eyes. Whatever you do, <u>don't</u> look down over the chasm below you.

That approach is probably particularly significant to me, because in some circumstances I have a problem with heights. It is a bit ironic that the Lord should, as it were, have made me the leader of teams going into some of the highest mountains in the world, and yet I do not always like high places. I get very dizzy going up ladders these days. I think the whole thing stems from my days in London some twenty or thirty years ago, when I was doing something to a gutter on a house; a bird flew out from underneath, the ladder wobbled and I very nearly fell. From that moment, I have always been very dubious about going up ladders, only doing so if I really must. Certainly, going across Chinese rope bridges is a big, big 'no-no' for me unless it is absolutely essential. But I have learnt over the years that sometimes the Lord takes those things that are a weakness, or a problem to us, and shows *his* strength and *his* glory. I think this is how the Lord ensures that whatever is achieved is done in his strength, in his way, and in his time.

In the world's economy, if you were a management consultant and you were appointing someone to lead teams through to some of the highest places in the world, you would make sure that the leader was not someone who had occasional vertigo, etc. But the Lord often does things in the reverse way to the world. I am convinced it is because he does not share his glory with anyone. He likes to take the weak things of the world and make them something beautiful for himself.

In 1998, on one of the preparation visits that we call 'reccies', we were going along one of these famous high and dangerous mountain roads when we came across an enormous blockage of rubble strewn across the way in front of us. Huge rocks, weighing many hundreds of tons, formed a great pile. Inevitably, a big hold-up resulted, as the convoy of vehicles was compelled to stop. We wandered several miles down the road, to reach a point where we could see what was happening. There we were presented with the most extraordinary sight. Chinese workers were walking along, pushing wheelbarrows full of dynamite; the little cardboard boxes they were wheeling around carried signs that said 'Danger'. One guy pushing his wheelbarrow had an enormous cigarette hanging out of the side of his mouth. I am sure someone will tell me that explosives are not dangerous without a detonator of some kind, but I still found it bizarre to see someone so close to so much potential disaster.

Dynamite seems to be freely available in that part of the world because there are so many blockages on the road, and the favourite way is to just come along with lots of sticks of it, put it in the side, and have an almighty explosion to pave the way forward. The only problem with letting off all these bangs is that the noise and vibration echoes down through the valleys and across the mountains, and it seems to shake the whole area. At times, we have been looking ahead with our binoculars to where they are clearing the road, only to find other rocks coming down on top of us where it has rocked the mountain behind, causing other boulders to rain down around us. I am not sure which is worse: the dangers of a natural rock fall, or the dangers resulting from those who are trying to clear it.

Many people in these very remote regions are very poor, and they find all sorts of ways of supplementing their income. I would not say it was prevalent, nor that it was a normal situation, but we have come across times when people have actually deliberately created landslides across the road. When your jeep or coach comes to a halt, you might find a group of very 'helpful' local people eager to help you out and 'shift it for a small consideration'. Usually, when this happens, the price is the equivalent of a couple of pounds. The same thing has been known to occur on wooden bridges, where some of the planks in strategic places seem to be mysteriously 'missing', only to reappear when an appropriate 'toll' has been paid. Whilst one does not condone such action, I have to say that I do have a bit of a soft heart for these local people trying to scrape a decent living. I guess one can always, to some extent, understand their actions, even if one does not agree with them.

Chapter Three

Culture Shock

Fishing, Tibetan style

In 1999, my brother, Keith, with Glyn and several others, were surveying an area further up-river from Dengke in a village called Bengda. Amongst other things, they were investigating the possibilities for eco-tourism. My brother had taken his fishing rods with him and was sitting by the Yangtze River to see whether it would be feasible for future visitors to fish. He was fishing in traditional style with a simple float and one hook, but without a lot of success it must be said. At that point some Tibetans turned up and announced that there were easier ways of getting fish.

Something which looked like a beer bottle was filled with some sort of explosive, and a wick was inserted in the end. Then a guy, who had been freely smoking, got hold of the bottle, took the cigarette out of his mouth and lit the fuse. After a brief pause, he lobbed the bottle into the Yangtze, and it disappeared from view. Seconds later a huge explosion went up, echoing all around the valley. Soon after that, dead or stunned fish were to be seen floating down the river, at which point some little naked Tibetan lads leapt in and started swimming furiously to catch the fish in their teeth and bring them back to shore. "That's how we do it in Tibet," announced the guy, who was looking more and more like an old-fashioned Marlborough cigarette advert.

Another key member of the same group that investigated the Bengda Region in 1999, who had been with me on earlier expeditions, was John Studley, a dedicated forester. He has produced some fascinating material, which you can find on the web. (See Appendix H.) John is one of the most hardworking people I know. I shall never forget a moment in 1995, before we had left Dengke for the journey home, when he presented me with a typed, 50 plus page report of his forestry findings. "How did you manage that?" I asked in disbelief.

"I've got a battery powered printer attached to the laptop," came the reply. I can only assume that, with colleagues, he had been working through the night to complete his brilliant treatise!

Whilst on the theme of dedication, I must mention the name of Peter Gunner. Peter is an 'engineering farmer'. He is quiet, unassuming, self-deprecating, and one of life's great pessimists. But I wonder where would we be without his generosity, kindness and sensitivity. I often tell new team members, "If I were stuck up a mountain in a snow storm in Tibet and I had just one choice of companion, it would be Peter. He is my best practical engineer." I quote the well-known saying: 'Two men look out from prison bars; one sees mud, the other sees stars.' When I see the long-term vision, Peter wisely observes the short-term difficulties. I think the reason we have been thrown together, from time to time, is that in the Lord's economy it is patently obvious we need each other!

Mutinies and rip-offs
It was back in 1987 when I first set foot on Chinese soil. That was in Beijing. On arrival, the luggage was lost and damaged. I can remember standing beside the carousel, waiting for it to appear, when a friendly official from the British Embassy, who also turned out to be a Christian, laughed and joked with me, saying, "Welcome to China", in a very ironic way. He intimated that our adventures had only just begun in terms of bureaucracy, hassle and all the problems that any traveller to China can identify with. He said something which turned out to be very prophetic at the time, namely that, "The Lord will always work out your problems in due time." He said that the exciting thing is to 'let go and let God'. He told us that his frequent prayer was: "How are you going to sort this one out, Lord? Surprise me."

Over the years, these surprises seem to have become larger and more frequent. Soon after the luggage incident at the airport, I was in a meeting with a whole group of other people planning the hovercraft expedition to China. We were sat in a room with a lot of high officials. What they did not know was that in our team we had a fluent Chinese speaker, a good Christian friend from the Norwegian Embassy. We sat round discussing the support costs for taking a hovercraft up the Yangtze. The price came out something like half a million pounds. (My notes indicate £481,576, including £191,077 for 'special permission' fees.) They announced the overall figure after we had been sitting around in a circle for two or three hours deep in discussion, with an interpreter between us sending messages backwards and forwards. When the quotation was delivered, we fell about laughing. We said to them, "Well, we are sure this is a very fair figure," (tongue in cheek) "but we just haven't got that sort of money, nowhere near it. We are a small private group of individuals." Anyway, the discussions went on for several more hours, backwards and forwards, backwards and forwards. Right at the very end, our man who could speak fluent Chinese, suddenly spoke to the Chinese across the room. Of course, they nearly fell off their chairs (in fact, I think one guy actually did) with shock. They rapidly realised that all the little private discussions, presumably about how they were going to 'maximise profit', had all been heard and understood. Thereafter, the discussion took a different tack and things became a bit more realistic.

In 1990 we were still deep in discussion with officials, this time in Chengdu. I was the lead negotiator for the British Hovercraft Expedition. I can remember getting more and more frustrated with the way that one particular official was trying to cheat us, adding things on to the bill all the way through. I am a very calm, placid sort of person when it comes to negotiations, but after several hours of this I was getting increasingly frustrated. So I thought, how can I change this conversation around to inject some reality into the situation? So what did I do? Basically, it was a hot day, so I took my shirt off in the middle of the negotiations and threw it into the middle of the floor. The whole conversation stopped. Everyone looked shocked, including Lily the interpreter. "What did you do that for?" she said. "Everyone is asking."

"Well, in my country we have a saying: 'Why don't you take my shirt as well?'"

At that point everyone fell about laughing, and once again we began to get back to a more realistic figure in our negotiations.

This problem of corruption and being ripped-off is something which occurs time and time again. Learning to deal with it is difficult. That is not to say that all officials are corrupt, certainly not. Some of the kindest people I know actually hold quite high office. But one has to face the fact that problems like this arise on a regular basis. On the hovercraft expedition, for example, when we were bringing in solar-powered fridges for keeping vaccines cool, one official quite blatantly wanted us to give him one to keep his beer cold. We said quite clearly to him, "No way. This equipment has been given for charitable purposes. 'Charitable purposes' does not include keeping your lager at an appropriate temperature."

Likewise, mutinies on mountains are quite common, particularly involving lorry drivers. These guys have become the bane of my life in China. On the hovercraft expedition I can remember one lorry driver leaping out and refusing to drive on a very icy patch high up in a snow-storm, on the top of a mountain; even allowing the lorry to inch forward, out of control and without someone at the helm. He had decided it was too dangerous. We pointed out that it would be even more dangerous to try and turn a huge lorry around on an icy precipice. In the end we managed to persuade him to keep going, though I think the main motive was to get more money.

In 1995 we were in Dengke, happily doing our charitable work, when a nameless official took me aside and told me that there would be no more meals provided for us after Saturday. I asked why this was so, when we had long ago negotiated a fixed-price contract, and everything was included. He said, "No discussion! More money is now required." This seems to be a favourite trick: get to somewhere very remote where the customer cannot do much about it, then suddenly make a demand for money, knowing that they are in a helpless situation.

I looked the official in the eye and said, "I believe in fairness. We took a long time negotiating this contract, and a deal is a deal. You can't suddenly start adding extra money on top of things now. The local people have given us such a huge and warm welcome here in the village, and many, many people have come to me and welcomed us into their homes. As far as I'm concerned, I'm prepared to take the whole of my team and go and live with the ordinary people in the village. In fact, we'd quite enjoy it."

The official was not quite sure how to take this. I could almost hear his mind ticking over as he thought, "Is this guy for real or not?" I think he realised I was not joking. In fact, I talked to the team and said to them later that evening, "Get prepared. We might actually be living in very simple houses with the local people after Saturday." Anyway, I stood my ground and they decided not to call my bluff. As it turned out, I think that on Sunday the meal was twice the size of that on Saturday. The point had been made —we were not going to be ripped off.

Likewise, having trouble with bus drivers seems to be a perennial problem. The 1999 expedition provides a case in point. Prior to leaving Chengdu, I negotiated with the providers of transport that new tyres would be put on all the vehicles, so as to reduce the danger on the very difficult roads that we knew we would experience in the mountains. A promise was made that new tyres would be put on at some point not too far into the start of the journey, so that when we got to the really difficult passes we would have the maximum safety margin. True to form however, when we were on top of a mountain in the far west of Sichuan, a number of the tyres blew out, and we found ourselves stranded in very difficult terrain. When we then discovered that the tyres which had failed were the very old and damaged ones that we had objected to in the first place, quite naturally I was not very impressed! They had lied about changing them. The fact that I was indignant seemed to infuriate the drivers, who threatened to walk out on us, turn round and drive back, leaving us on the mountainside. At this point I said, "You're not going anywhere, other than forward. If necessary we will all take a sleep behind the coach and lie down in the sunshine until you come to your senses."

Once again, it was a question of standing firm and not being bullied by people who have quite a bit of power over you when you are way away from city centres. Eventually, things calmed down. Tyres were repaired, and we carried on. Much later, we insisted on getting some money back for the tyres that we had paid to have changed. Mutinies by drivers seem to be par for the course in this part of China and Tibet.

Fun and laughter
Happily, in between the serious moments come numerous times of laughter and fun, like the time when our interpreters fell into fits of

mirth as we were ordering Tibetan horses. After jokingly threatening my 'Chinese daughter' with the severest of punishments if she did not 'spill the beans' and interpret, I dragged out of her that one of our larger team members (I will spare his blushes) was about to be charged twice as much as the rest of us because, "He weighs twice as much." I hope the horse got twice as much hay!

Similarly, the same team member has dined out many times on the story of his urgent fax. He was in a Chengdu hotel when the phone rang and a young girl asked if he wanted his 'message'. "Yes", he said, "now, and very urgently." Minutes later the door rang and after a few moments of a rather curious conversation he realised she had confused 'urgent message' with 'urgent massage'. She left rather hurriedly.

Getting unsolicited phone calls in hotels is par for the course in Chengdu, and my team fell about laughing in the middle of a meeting when a similar type of call interrupted our daily prayer time. All the more reason to pray, of course!

In Dengke, I once playfully pinched one of Val Thomson's sweets, and was chased down the corridor of the government hostel, only to trip up and land in a heap on the floor, clutching a painful arm. Just for a joke, I got one of our doctors to strap me up, as if I had broken it. The following morning, Val came down to breakfast and (being the kind, caring person that she is) spotted my arm and was desperately contrite. Being a physio, she asked me to try various very gentle movements with my fingers, to see if she could assess the level of damage. I played along with this until, unable to contain myself any more, I started moving my whole arm in a massive 'royal wave'. Eventually, she saw the joke...... I think. Lily, my 'Chinese daughter' was not impressed, and I got a severe telling off. OK, I will try to behave better in the future.

In the Project Dengke of 1992 we used to be awakened by loud-speakers (from somewhere down our corridor) blasting out what we assumed to be radio propaganda. "Don't worry, boss", one of our electricians, Grant Freeman, said. "I'll fix it." Next morning, the dulcet tones lasted about ten seconds before spluttering into silence, only to start up again ten minutes later. "Don't worry, boss, I will *really* fix it for tomorrow morning." And he did! I do not know how he did it, but the blissful quietness was deafening. One needs one's sleep, especially as the dogs of all shapes and sizes seem to wake up at night and howl endlessly. This was a problem not wasted on Andrew Sneller, whose professional quantity surveying skills were augmented by becoming chief dog disperser, complete with a bag of bones —or was it stones? John Whatmore had earlier failed the audition for this role, having been bitten on the backside, when wearing shorts, by a baby dog who had 'lost the plot'. Apparently, John had told a team member something like, "If you show them you are not scared, don't look them in the eye, and march boldly through the middle of them, they will leave you alone!" He subsequently found out that it works fine for adult dogs, but not puppies. Ouch! Anyway, John is a great producer and has made some fine TV programmes, as have Mike Pritchard, Peter Coulson and Keith Hopper.

God's timing is always perfect.
When leading expeditions in China and Tibet, I have often been faced with what seemed at the time to be impossible situations, where nothing but a miracle would do. When you are far away from the main cities you cannot fall back upon all the things that we rely on in everyday life in the West. For example, you cannot just phone up and negotiate. You cannot, as it were, put pressure on people to resolve a problem. It is much easier in the West to resolve problems by human ingenuity and by experience, and by knowing how to handle a particular situation. The complexities of different cultures, of corruption, of intransigence, and of suspicion make things very, very difficult in China and Tibet. In 1995, for example, despite the fact that we had sent all our equipment, and the parts for a bridge, across the world in a container many, many weeks in advance of the main expedition, it did not mean that everything was going to arrive on time, and without problems. In fact, what happened was that our container, full of all our kit, and all the parts described, got stuck, first in Hong Kong and then in Shenzhen. Having spent over two years painstakingly preparing that particular project, you can imagine the frustration and agony of having all the expedition equipment, as well as £50,000 of medicines and humanitarian goods, impounded for nearly two months.

Eventually it was released, but only after intervention by the British Embassy *and* the Assistant British Trade Commissioner, *and* the Governor of Sichuan Province *and* the Chairman of Leicestershire County Council. We shall never know the real reason for the Customs intransigence in refusing to allow the container to continue its journey across China to Chengdu, where we were to open it up and prepare for our journey into the mountains. Were the Customs holding out for a bribe? Were they genuinely worried that we would sell the goods on the black market? Your guess is as good as mine. All I know is that it nearly wrecked our whole expedition. They even had the cheek to charge us over £1,000 as a 'tax' on very old computers that we were giving away, despite documents from British Customs that they were zero-rated. In addition, they held on for nearly four months to the £1,550 of a so-called 'deposit' on goods being returned to the UK, which we had paid them on the way in. Presumably, someone made a handsome profit on the interest.

Whilst all the equipment was impounded in Shenzhen, the team I had assembled arrived in China from all over the world. We set up base in Chengdu —around forty people of nine different nationalities. We met together, and we prayed together, realising the biggest problem to be resolved was that all the equipment was stuck, hundreds of miles away, out of our control. We prayed very much for wisdom, and as leader I knew I had some difficult decisions to make. Eventually, I decided that I would take the team into the mountains, as a step of faith, without our equipment, and without knowing what would happen in the future. For all I knew, I would be taking an international team way out into the wilds of Western Sichuan, only to find that we could do nothing when we arrived in Dengke. This was a huge challenge, and a huge worry, but somehow, deep in my soul, I knew it was the right decision. When we did arrive in Dengke, after four or five days journey, we set about some of the preliminary tasks that we could begin without all our main equipment. After a few days, we knew that the clock was ticking down, and if we were going to, for example, build the bridge we had planned, we would need that equipment very, very soon. Again, it was a deeply worrying time, and we agonised, each one of us, in prayer. Eventually, it got to the point where it seemed as though the team had divided into two camps. One group was saying that the Lord was telling us that we were in Dengke for a different purpose, and that we had to adjust to the current situation and get on with the new tasks, which he would give us. The other half of the team was saying that we should hold on in faith, believing that what God had started, he would finish, and that the equipment would arrive in time. Ultimately, of course, the decision as to which direction to take falls on the leader. The buck stopped with me. I prayed very much, and I can remember waking up in the night, very troubled —and I began reading various scriptures. Then a very quiet peace came over me, and I knew what the Lord was telling me. The following day, I told the team that I felt confident that things were going to work out the way that had been originally planned, and that the equipment would come through to us. The whole team were with me, and we trusted together, knowing that this might look very, very foolish in the eyes of the world.

We had a satellite telephone, but because we did not have the main generator, we could not operate the power supply correctly. As we connected it up, using the village power supply, there was one sentence of information which came through, saying that Customs had released the equipment, which was on its way. Then the whole system blew up because there was a power surge, or a change of voltage, and the electronics just could not cope with it. That was it. End of communication! But just enough information got through for us to know that our prayers had been answered. We were right out on a limb. We had taken that step of faith; the Lord had honoured it. The equipment was on its way. Time and again in Tibet and China we have found that the Lord works this way.

Repeatedly, we have found that he sends us back to basics, back to the place of prayer and trust. The really amazing thing was that the lorry turned up in the compound in Dengke almost to the last minute on the last day it would have been conceivable for us to be able to finish the project in the way planned. But it did arrive, amidst great rejoicing, and we did complete the project. But it was 'right down to the wire'. In fact the last part of the operation (Mike Wisheart tightening some bolts) was carried out with minutes to spare before we left for home some weeks later. About to leave, we sat in the bus looking at our watches and tapping our fingers —right up to the moment he rushed back down the mountain and jumped wearily inside the vehicle. A little later, we passed the brightest and most brilliant rainbow I have ever seen, arcing down over the area where we had struggled and served: symbolic perhaps? God loves, cares and keeps his promises.

Chapter Four

'The Rough with the Smooth'
—Some Agonies of Leadership

All the expeditions I have led have been rough and tough. But then, front line action for the Lord always is. Although I have headed up many teams over the years, I have always been careful to promise each and every member that they will definitely be on an expedition, not a picnic, and that everybody would return as different people from those who had set out. They would have an adventure they would never forget.

The expedition in 1999 was no exception. It took two years of really hard, painstaking planning to get under way, which is about the average time all the other expeditions have taken as well. I quite regularly get up at six o'clock in the morning, have a cup of tea, pray, switch the computer on and work hard for several hours before breakfast. To prepare for an expedition, this needs to go on for many months, indeed years, in order to get to the place where everything is ready to roll.

The combination of high altitude and extremely dangerous roads, lack of sleep, and the fact that we are going right to the heart of the spiritual 'enemy'—Satan, the one who the Bible makes clear is opposed to the work of God—does not endear us to that same enemy. By 'enemy', of course, I do *not* mean people. We love all the people we meet on our expeditions, and we have peace in our hearts. No—I mean the spiritual enemy whose attacks our Lord Jesus Christ had to endure; the enemy that Jesus defeated on the cross.

Where did you say you are?

Thankfully, although we have had many exciting adventures, we have not had to deal with too many potentially life or death situations concerning the health of team members. The only exceptions were perhaps in 1992 when Barbara Forbes had a severe reaction to medication, and in 1999 when we had to deal with a possible precursor to a heart attack, concerning Jack Sharples. In the latter case, he had keeled over during an evening team meeting, and the medical team told me I HAD to get him out. Both Jack and I had our doubts about such a radical step, but I felt that, for the sake of Jack and his family, I had to bow to the doctors' judgement. Even this incident had its lighter moments, however. We used the satellite phone to contact the insurers, who claimed they could get 'anyone, anywhere, home in forty-eight hours', or some such similar boast.

The conversation went something like this:

"Where are you? Never heard of it. Don't worry, our people in Beijing will know."

"Beijing here, where are you? Never heard of it. Don't worry — our medical people will know."

"Medical team here. Where are you? Never heard of it. You had better give us longitude and latitude. Ah! Now we see it. Don't worry we can get a helicopter to you within hours."

"Sorry, they can't get a helicopter in —too high, too remote. An ambulance is on its way."

To give them their due, a rather smart ambulance and crew got to us within two and a half days by travelling non-stop through the night. As Jack seemed to be OK, some of the team kept his spirits up by telling him what fantastic TV pictures and story a helicopter rescue would make. Being carted off in an ambulance, however, did not quite have the same ambience. On getting back home, Jack was pronounced as being perfectly OK —but we cannot blame the doctors for being careful and diligent. I often joke to Jack that maybe the real reason he passed out was due to Rob Alcock. Rob had an eating problem which meant he would come in half way through a meeting and stoke up the ancient, leaky, rusty, solid fuel, stove with wood and dried Yak dung. This was so he could warm up his baked beans in a wok. I noticed, consequently, that whenever the fire was raging everyone got sleepy and started nodding off, irrespective of who was holding forth in the meeting. Could it be a case of oxygen starvation or even carbon monoxide poisoning? Probably not —but it makes a good story.

Protection

Over the years, I have become convinced, that despite my vulnerability from a personal and spiritual perspective, I have been protected as a team leader in a very special way. I am sure this has happened many times, but perhaps in 1999 I was very acutely aware of it. I appointed various departmental leaders in medical, education, eco-tourism and engineering etc. But the Lord himself did something very remarkable, that I certainly could not do. He promoted a small group of my team to be what I describe as 'sons and daughters of encouragement'. It seems as though he gave this little group a precious insight into the pressures and loneliness I bore, and indeed, still bear, as a leader having to take difficult and unpopular decisions. It seemed as though there was a little, loyal group that formed around me, like a ring of angels, constantly sharing words and deeds of encouragement from the Lord. How I have thanked God for them over the years; and how much I needed them then and will need them in the future. I am reminded of these verses of Scripture:

Your love has given me great joy and encouragement, because you, brother, have refreshed the hearts of the saints *(Philemon v. 7)*

May the God who gives endurance and encouragement, give you a spirit of unity among yourselves as you follow Christ Jesus, so that with one heart and mouth you may glorify the God and Father of our Lord Jesus Christ *(Romans 15:5,6).*

Different leaders lead their teams in different ways. Everybody has their own style and way of doing things. I guess I learnt my way of doing things having been deputy leader to Squadron Leader Mike Cole in the 1990 Hovercraft Expedition. The important thing is to be focussed on what you are doing and to be aware of those around you, and your team, their strengths and their weaknesses; and also to walk carefully with the Lord. All of this is easy to say, but very hard to put into practice. To quote Mike: "avoid taking a firm grasp of the non-essentials."

When you are in very remote, dangerous and difficult situations, important decisions have to be made, which really only one person can make. Just like somebody driving a coach, with the safety of all the passengers in his hands, he has to make individual split-second decisions. Similarly, just as in the case of the pilot of an aeroplane, or somebody piloting a boat, you cannot really have a consensus for all the decisions that need to be made. Obviously, a wise leader listens very carefully to what people around him say, but at the end of the day, you can only have one captain of a ship. And that is the way it is with expeditions in China and Tibet.

Very often, groups of people divide in their opinions, taking different directions. Somebody has to give clear leadership. My style has been to listen carefully to what people say, and when everybody has had their say, and I have pondered and prayed, I then make the decision, which may or may not be in line with the consensus.

I am not suggesting this is necessarily the way that everybody should lead projects, just that I think this is the right way for me and for the teams that I have been involved with. But it does not come easily, and it comes at great cost. Every time I have come back from leading teams in China, I have returned exhausted. But, most importantly, I have felt comfortable with myself, and with my Lord, and in the direction that I had led people. This has been despite knowing that I have made decisions that people have not agreed with, and knowing that I have had to be unpopular at times. I guess this is the agony of leadership with which each and every pioneer has to come to terms. Church leaders will no doubt be quietly nodding and empathising at this point.

Taking difficult decisions in Tibet and China is even trickier when one has to deal with all the encumbrances, controversies and brickbats; but it is all worth it.

Chapter Five

Champagne Moments

Recruiting team members

People have often asked me, 'How do you get members on your team? Do you put out advertisements? Do you go round Institutes and churches and places, asking for people to join you?' The answer is that I cannot recall ever directly advertising for anyone to come on any expedition. It seems as though the word goes around, and people learn about things through the grapevine, so to speak, phoning me, and contacting me in amazing ways. We always seem to end up with a very balanced and strong team, who are up to the task required for a particular expedition in a particular year. That does not mean to say I have not had agonies sometimes, wondering whether we are going to get it all together in time. One example of this was when, in 1995, I thought we had recruited some eye surgeons from the United States. Over the months, I had listened to their requirements for equipment and had gone round painstakingly getting bits of kit together from various companies. Leica, for example, had promised us £30,000 worth of operating microscope, suitable for what these eye surgeons required. Having spent a long time obtaining the equipment, imagine my despair when I found out at the last minute that the American group could not join us. Several people said to me, "It will be impossible now to get somebody suitable, because surgeons need to get replacement people in post to take over their surgery. They need locums, and they also need to make special arrangements within their hospitals." So the word went out for people supporting us to pray. Imagine my surprise when, early one morning, I had a phone call from a guy who said, "Hello, you won't know me, I'm an eye surgeon. I was going to Burma, but that has been cancelled at the last minute. I've been told that you're looking for an eye surgeon, and the dates seem to tie up with what you have in mind." Naturally, I was delighted, and even more delighted and staggered when he went on to say, "Oh, by the way, I have a friend who is also an eye surgeon. Could you use him as well?"

I suppose I should not have been surprised at the power of prayer, but I guess I was! I put the phone down, and then within a few minutes I had another phone call. And the guy at the other end said, "Hello, you won't know me; I'm an eye surgeon." The third one was totally unconnected to the first two, so once again I was totally amazed. They had all heard through the grapevine that we needed eye surgeons, and were offering their services.

So man's impossibilities became God's opportunities as we responded to such situations in prayer. I was in a great state of exhilaration and drove in to work that morning with a real smile on my face. As I was driving along, I passed Colin Garner, a colleague who was to come with me on the expedition. I wound down the window and said, "Hey, you won't believe this, but we've got three eye surgeons for Dengke", and dashed off.

A little later on that morning, I had an email from Colin on my desk computer saying: 'I didn't know they needed three-eye surgery in Dengke.' I responded: 'Yes, I know they are three-eyed surgeons, but they are having a bit of trouble with their ministry at the moment. No-one will give them a break, so I'm going to give it to them, in Dengke!'

Once again this helps to illustrate one of the essential requirements for being on one of my expeditions: a good sense of humour. Incidentally, I also look for a very high level of commitment —Commitment with a very big capital C. When I travel around the country and give talks about expeditions and adventures, I quite often get people come up to me at the end, offering their services. Of course, in the exhilaration of an after-meeting, people are all fired up and keen to help, which is very good of them, and very understandable. But we need more than people who are just temporarily inspired by seeing some adventure packed slides or video. Using a technique which I got from

Mike Cole, I deliberately do not tell people too much about myself when they chat to me in such situations. I very often will not give them a business card or even a leaflet with my name and address on (unless they specifically ask). The idea is to test their commitment over a period of days or weeks. Basically, they have to decide how they are going to contact me. If they are really committed, the first step will be for them to try hard to find out what my address is and where I came from. It is like a first hurdle, to see whether someone can actually reach me and get to me, even though they do not know my address.

One person who amazes me with her commitment to expedition membership, is June Fish, our hearing specialist. You can read her personal story later. Early one Saturday morning, back in 1995, I had a phone call. June asked about our expeditions, what we did and whether she could be of service. I explained basically what it was all about, saying, "As a matter of fact there's going to be a meeting today at Loughborough University for all those who are interested. I suppose it's a bit much to ask you this, but if you could have got up here today then we could have given you a complete run-down on all that's involved."

She immediately set about contacting a friend of mine, John Whatmore, who was also going to the meeting, to get a lift, and to arrive at the meeting, even though she had only known about it minutes before. To me, this illustrates the ideal sort of commitment, and what we look for in team membership. She had probably got something else lined up for the day, but dropped everything, was totally focussed, and was completely determined to come and meet the team and find out more. That total spiritual, mental and physical commitment that I look for is symptomatic of what I believe is God's call on our lives. I also owe it to June for encouraging Andrea (a drama teacher from the USA) to come on the 1999 expedition. Both their amazing stories are shared in Chapters 7 and 9.

When you are halfway up a mountain with a wheel off a lorry, or up to your axles in mud, or in the middle of a snowstorm, or caught in a snow slide or an earthquake, the last thing you want are people who are uncommitted; people who turn round and say 'Mum, I want to go home.' Rather, we want people who know their calling, and who roll their sleeves up and get stuck in, ready for the unexpected, from whatever direction it might come.

In 1999, the last minute need was for a dentist. Once again, I had other dentists lined up for the project, but at the last ditch people had to pull out. Again, I had commitment from various companies with equipment and supplies, but no dentist to operate and use them. Just before the expedition, I went to a prayer meeting at Richard Meredith's house to support student work. We spent the evening praying in support of the work at Loughborough University. At the end of it Richard said, "I believe you are off on an expedition soon. What can we pray for?"

"Well," I said, "there's one particular need, and that's for a dentist."

"OK," he said, "let's do it." And we spent some moments praying for that particular need. Within a day or two following that prayer meeting, Jill Gibson (or a friend of hers) contacted me, to enquire more about the work in the mountains. Jill is a qualified dentist. So one thing led to another, and she came with us, another 'trophy of grace'.

Abba, Father

Christians are very familiar with the term 'Abba'. It is an Aramaic word used by Jesus, meaning 'dearest father' or 'daddy'. It is an intimate word, a very loving word, which we find in the Bible to describe that special relationship we can have with our Father God. You can imagine my surprise when this particular word cropped up in another context. June Fish had been testing a number of children for hearing deficiencies. There was one particular little urchin girl in a brown jacket, who had been deaf almost from birth. When she was tested, it was clear that she could not hear. The doctors and June ministered to her in different ways, and June fitted her with a little hearing aid. It was a moment of pure joy when the little girl could hear for the very first time. She was sitting on her dad's knee, and her face lit up when her father whispered a word to her and she repeated it. That word was 'Abba'. She was saying, "Abba, Abba." I called it a 'champagne moment'. The Khamba Tibetan dialect word for 'daddy' is 'abba', and for me it was very, very symbolic. It reminded me of our Father God; it reminded me of the intimate relationship we can have with him through Jesus Christ his Son; and it reminded me that God's love extends even to these dear people in this extremely remote village.

Satellite links

Other 'champagne moments' have included the first flow of clean water into the village; blind patients jumping for joy at eyesight being restored; and unusual things happening when you least expect them. One of these involved our communication links. On the first occasion we took a satellite phone to Dengke, it required a lot of setting up. We pointed the large dish in the appropriate direction and plugged in the electronics. Excitedly, we dialled a UK number to test the system when a voice, clear as a bell, came through the headset, "Hi, this is Matthew."

As I had not dialled a 'Matthew' I instinctively replied, "Matthew who?"

"Matthew, your son, remember?" came a bewildered response.

What had happened was that I had not completed my dial-out procedure by pressing 'enter', and in the meantime, by coincidence, my eldest son was trying to ring me. It was quite a shock, but very welcome! These satellite phones seem to shrink in size year by year. Our current version is like a small laptop computer and, instead of a dish, the small lid is pointed, appropriately, up to the sky. Likewise, we have recently been field trialling a palm-top computer system linked to a miniature radio transmitter that beams up to passing low level satellites. This 'forward and store' email system can be used even when surrounded by mountains and, remarkably, does not require any positioning of a dish or aerial.

Unlikely liaisons

One thing I have learned about working in China and Tibet is always to be ready for the unexpected, and grasp opportunities when they arise.

On one occasion, when I was being seen off at Chengdu airport, Lily grabbed my arm and said, "Guess what? Over there is one of China's biggest rock bands called 'Black Panther'."

Intrigued, I said, "Let's go and chat to them. You can translate!"

"No way."

"You're joking, surely you haven't gone all weak kneed and star struck at your age!"

"No, I'm not coming, but I will write down an introduction for you." So I strolled over, only to find that the lead singer, Yong, spoke perfect English. They were relaxed and affable, and asked me why I came to China so often. They seemed genuinely amazed at the charity adventures I related to them.

"Ring me on this number next time you pass through Beijing," Yong said, passing me a slip of paper. "I would like to hear more about your work, and would like you to be our guest at a big concert in the Olympic Stadium." Some months later I made that phone call and was met at Beijing airport, and had my bags carried through a swell of fans by China's big 'heart throb', whose band has sold over 100 million records. I must admit it was both good fun and bizarre having a mass of people eyeing me up and down and no doubt assuming the 'old guy' was a famous Western rock star. Well, one thing has led to another since then including unique opportunities to share the reason for 'the hope within me'. I also arranged for BP to perform their first Western open air concert in Leicester Square, London, in February 1998. This was part of a Charity Chinese New Year event sponsored by Richard Branson and the traders in China Town. As a 'thank you', BP have since re-recorded one of their most famous hits as a tribute song to us using lyrics written by one of the west's most famous drummers, Bobby Graham. I must confess to a few emotional moments when I first played the tape when it arrived in my post, out of the blue, one Monday morning. The touching words are in Appendix C. The actual song can be found on our website. (See Appendix H.)

A vision for the future
People often ask me why I am drawn back to the little village of Dengke. Well, I suppose first and foremost it is a 'calling' that motivates me to return and to care and share with the local people; and obviously, as a Christian, I want to share all that I have. The modern term for this is, I suppose, 'holistic ministry'.

Sharing all that we have would include food, would include technology, would include the love and care that is denied to some, and of course it would include sharing the living faith which is deep within us as Christians. But I believe the Lord has also given us, and given me in particular perhaps, a vision for the future. There are no known Christians in this area, and certainly no known Christians in the village of Dengke. And yet there, in the centre, to the side of the high street, there is a building that (if rebuilt) could be used as a legally registered church, and I guess would enable all, if not a large proportion, of the village to gather for worship if they came to the Lord one day. So I get drawn whenever I return to the village, to wander down to this derelict building. It was once, I believe, some sort of entertainment centre or maybe a cinema, or a meeting point for the Chinese army when they were there in the 1950s. It is one of the biggest buildings in the town. It is locked and chained up. But going round the side of it, one can just about climb up and look through some cracks in one of the wooden doors and see the dusty area inside. Likewise, you can see the stage at one end. Up until the visit in 1999, one could see rows and rows of chairs but these have now been moved, so there is just dusty ground in their place. I have always had this feeling, deep in my heart, that one day the whole village will turn to the Lord, and this place could become a church in the sense of a building where they could gather together to sing praises to God. I often quietly pray that in the Lord's time the miracle will be wrought.

At the moment, the only obvious religion in Dengke is Buddhism. At the end of the main high street is the temple, and outside are the prayer drums. People continuously walk round and round turning the drums, seeking to earn favour. Great banks of prayer flags flap in the wind to represent the prayers of the people. Sometimes one sees, mainly elderly, people sitting by the side of the road, turning their prayer wheels, sometimes quietly chanting to themselves. The emphasis is very much on doing things to earn favour, whether turning wheels or flying flags. This is the opposite of what we believe in the Christian religion. We can earn nothing by 'doing things'. Our salvation is in Jesus alone and trusting in him and in his grace. Even our goodness is as filthy rags. We just have to throw ourselves upon his mercy and accept the wonderful promise of eternal life that he has given us as we turn from our sins and follow him.

End of the beginning or beginning of the end?

William Carey once wrote, 'Expect great things from God, Attempt great things for God.' That is just as true today as it has been in the past —easy to say, of course, in a book, a sermon, or sitting watching the television. The trouble is we are all SO weak, and putting it into practice often seems like an impossible dream. Returning home from Project Dengke 99, I must admit I was totally drained! I said to my wife, "That's it, I have done my bit. It's time for others to take up the baton. I need the hassle of expedition leadership like I need a dose of salts —why am I putting myself through all this 'aggro' when I could have the easy life?" It had cost me copious amounts of time, serious money, and I had neglected my academic career…. What is more, I did not even like heights, etc., etc. The trouble is, of course, God had other plans! The vision for a Centre in Dengke kept coming back to me, time and time again. I could not escape. If I wanted spiritual peace I had to come to terms with the fact that my Maker was telling me I had not completed the task HE had set before me. Finally, he used dear enthusiastic friends, like Glyn Davies and John Owens, to encourage me to "stop messing about and move onwards."

Thus at relatively short notice, in October 2001, I was challenged to put together a small 'recce' (forward planning and feasibility) team to seek out the way forward.

A clear vision had been laid on our hearts to pursue the setting up of the International Friendship Centre, which seemed ridiculous but for the fact the Lord had reminded us, "…My ways are not your ways…." The Centre(s) would provide a base for active caring in a part of the world where there are no known believers. Thus, practical help and service could be expressed by small medical teams; at other times, engineering support; at other times, teaching in the local schools, etc. The idea was that, come what may, whoever finally made the Centre their base would always be ready to share the reason for the hope within them.

Because of the spiritual dimension associated with pursuing such objectives, we were expecting huge opposition during the recce, and the whole armoury of the devil's 'dirty tricks department' to be pointed straight at us. We sensed that whilst there would be those who would support us, there would be others who would not, and from whom we must disengage. In the event, it was clear that God had gone ahead of us (and just like the story in Joshua about a small group going into the promised land expecting 'giants' but finding the opposite), we found potentially awkward officials and leaders falling over themselves to welcome us back, and being co-operative. One friend with high connections, who shall remain anonymous, explained to me, with tears in his eyes, that he was embarrassed that sometimes his fellow countrymen tried to rip us off. When I suggested however that it would be better for him if I did not involve him in projects on an automatic basis he got quite agitated. "But you are my dear friend," he protested. "You must *always* involve me." —Quite something, for someone with a lot to lose.

Time after time, the Lord put us in contact with just the right people at just the right time. Even delays due to broken jeeps caused us to meet 'by chance' very senior officials on snowy, icy mountainsides, and they readily gave their endorsement to our proposals. The bottom line is that God opened the doors and did miraculous things for us. Against all expectations, we were offered, not one but two massive plots of land in Dengke AND Shiqu (the regional capital) on which to build our proposed Friendship Centres —free of charge.

The secret of success stemmed from events that took place before we embarked on the journey. Just prior to leaving, readings had been shared with us on successive mornings (independently, and without knowledge of our circumstances), that gave us great heart and encouragement to get on with it and ignore the doubters.

'Do two walk together, unless they have agreed to do so?' (Amos 3:3)

"The LORD is with me; I will not be afraid" (Psalm 118:6)

'For he will command his angels concerning you to guard you in all your ways' (Psalm 91:11)

"Rise up; this matter is in your hands....
Take courage and do it..." (Ezra 10:4)

Thus we believed God had spoken to our hearts to:
(a) Follow the vision for service he had given us.
(b) Believe that we would have travelling mercies.
(c) Not to walk (work with) those who do not share the same goals.

Believe me, this was like a breath of spiritual fresh air!

When we arrived in Shiqu (en route to Dengke) we were warmly greeted by a Regional Tibetan Governor called Kato. Do you remember the Peter Sellers *Pink Panther* films? "Not now Kato.... ahaaa...." If so, you will know why we smiled! Apologies to those who are completely mystified by my sense of humour at this point... but we move on. His Deputy was a Han Chinese called Mr Li. Both were wonderfully kind and accommodating, and said to me, "What size land are you looking for?" My instinct was to be cautious, and not to over-play my hand. I thought rapidly on my feet.... What would a small house stand on...? I blurted out: "5m x 10m".

"That's no good," said Kato. My heart sank, as I was thinking I had blown it. "Far too small," he continued. "You must have room to build AND expand!" At this point, we were whisked off on a tour of prime building sites, all around 70m x 70m. What is more, we were told they were totally free of charge! Next visit was across the moun-tains to Dengke. At this point the story becomes almost too incredible to believe —but believe you must! Where do you think we were taken, to be offered another 'Friendship Centre' land site? Yes, you guessed it: the place of prayer —next to the old cinema. I cannot begin to describe the deep feelings of being humbled before God, and utter amazement. I turned to Glyn and John and said, "What do we do now?" They just laughed, saying, "You have been praying for this for ten years —seems pretty obvious to us...."

What was that movie where someone said, 'Of all the bars in all the world...'? Casablanca? Of all the places in the village they could have offered.... Amazing! What is more, they said that they would knock the old building down free of charge, and give us the bricks. I know we should not be surprised by such things happening, but we are. The offer was later confirmed by Mr Li in a 'letter of intent'. We explained, as we always do, that we would keep within the limits of Chinese law. In fact, as Christians we have always believed that as guests in a foreign country being peaceful and law abiding is a witness in itself.

A few months later, in March 2002, following a tip-off from Pe-ter Anderson (who has been a wonderful friend and supporter over the years), I was able to meet, along with Martin Klopper and James Knapp, a Chinese lawyer in Beijing to discuss land legal matters. This 'legal eagle' had recently come into blessing through the witness of his girlfriend; and in a wonderful act of generosity offered to do the legal work free of charge. He felt that what we were doing would be of great benefit to the Chinese and Tibetan people, and this was his way of supporting. Later the same day, I also met some young producers from Central China TV (CCTV) whose stations have an audience of

1.2 billion. They explained that they were keen to do, "a proper documentary —not propaganda". Their idea is to follow the international goodwill aspects of setting up the Centre, and also show different groups from all over the world fund raising for a common cause. For us, this could be a wonderful witness as well as a means of getting sponsorship. Many companies are trying to get into China; I will happily wear their logo and t-shirt…. Anyone interested? Their name gets on television, and I get my Centre paid for!

So 'watch this space'. The story of Project Dengke is still unfolding. By the time you read these words, the legal documents may have been completed, and the next stage of fund raising and 'centre building' may have begun.

Maybe you will join us… perhaps you will be part of the story too….

PART TWO

Diaries of Adventure

Chapter Six

Sandra Watson's Story (1992)

The nasal, airport announcements guided us to the correct gate. The rising roar of the engines matched our excitement as, airborne, we flew over the Ardennes, the Alps and the Appalachians on the start of our journey of care and share — Project Dengke 92 — project of purpose, expedition of encouragement.

September 2 Hong Kong Airport (there must have been wheel marks on the roofs of nearby flats) was all air-conditioned, marble-floored efficiency; then out into the sticky chaos of taxi ranks and bus queues of heaving humanity squeezing into this part of Asia. One's senses were constantly assaulted by the strident street cries, the bartering, the arguing, the air laced with a whiff of acrid fumes, the dazzle of skyscrapers, of neon lights, and everywhere the 'people porridge', from the elegant affluence of the Peninsula Hotel to the back street shacks of plastic and tumble-down timber. Fashionflair females and telephone-talking brisk businessmen, school children and street traders provided uninterrupted movement.

Osborn Barracks, Hong Kong, was Hampshire with heat. Ghurkas guarded the gate, heavy booted, and British officers and army personnel appeared occasionally, mostly in civvies, tight with over-nourishment. Uniformed school children changed into T-shirts and shorts to play British games with British voices. Chinese *ayis* looked after the babies. This little replica bit of Britain, very much a 'sceptred isle' in the midst of a sea of tumultuous uncertainty, resounded to the monotonous call of the cricket, like a creaking board in steady need of oiling. Breakfast was egg and bacon.

The spotless underground system organised the buzz of people into queues that formed obediently at the painted-arrowed platform, where the train doors opened exactly. Most of the team took the humid, headaching journey by train to Guanzhou, beset by problems of long waits, long walks, dehydration, thieves and insistent beggars. The scenery slid past the windows from the twentieth century bustle and highways of Hong Kong and the New Territories, into the timelessness of the Chinese countryside; fields crammed together and cropped unbelievably tightly. Glassy paddy fields reflected stooping, straw-hatted farm workers methodically planting out rice. A punt in the middle of a small pond, one man sitting in the stern, another standing in the bows casting his net in a lazy arc over the still waters. From thence, the peeling paint plane into Chengdu. Others flew direct from Hong Kong and enjoyed a succession of gifts: a refreshment towel, a drink, perfume spray, bottles of pollen extract, and a good meal, all served by charming air hostesses who nurtured us into the beginnings of our form-filling routine.

September 3rd Chengdu; with its cloak of murky dust pollution, its steady swirl of cyclists like tributaries joining the main stream flow, with ankle-knocking pedals, interlocking wheels and unbelievably overloaded cargoes. Carpenters and painters, with tools of their trade strapped to their handlebars, waited to be hired as they lined the bridge. Everywhere, new imposing buildings reach to the sky, announcing new shopping malls and new hotels, the opening of tourism and private business, stockmarkets and free markets alongside flea markets and black markets, pedlar markets and florist shops on wheels. At times, a suggestion of a breeze would stir up the smog, and part the pollution to give shadows to the grey days. The people were mostly polite and friendly, smart and shrewd, many with second and third jobs. The shops were overstaffed, with under occupied, well-mannered personnel putting in hours of strenuous knitting, newspaper reading, card playing, tea drinking, or even sleeping between the occasional purchaser. The street sellers were much more expeditious in their urgency for customers.

The new airport breathed a calm kindliness of a gentle welcome before we were pitched through the doors to the open air meeting point, where we recognised John Whatmore. Chengdu boasted a new road into the city centre, past old rice fields and handcarts lit frugally by the irregular electricity supply. Bikes need no lights —as one Chinese student told me, when we stumbled down an unlit staircase; "Chinese people can see very well in the dark." From our hotel balcony we watched the trundling of wheelbarrows, filled with cement, down uneven planks for the ground floor of a new block. Eleven o'clock at night; many men hard at work, labouring to complete a task a cement lorry could have finished in a fraction of the time.

September 4 We packed into the bus at 5.30 a.m. Although dark, many folk were up, eating out or cycling to their work. The misty morning cleared to undimmed day. Men led bulky, grey, water buffalo by rope to their small fields. Bulging baskets of harvested sweetcorn and rice burdened the backs of their bowed bearers. The Chinese horn concerto played ad lib and ad infinitum, accompanying the forward movement of the bus and two lorries of equipment. We closed our eyes at the constant overtaking on blind bends on the first mountain pass, where we met our first traffic jam. We climbed out of the bus and saw a crowd up ahead. Some of our group went to investigate and witnessed a scuffle where police were beating up two resisting, handcuffed men. Blood flowed. Two lorries had gone over the edge, and large logs of timber lay beside the road. Cameras clicked, camcorders recorded, and as always in China the gathered crowd meted out noisy judgement. We moved on, edging round a hole —half the road had disappeared in a landslide, reminding us that here the terra was not so firma.

Woven straw mats carpeted the sides of the road; women raked and swept the sweet corn cobs or niblets, drying in the sun. Everywhere, we observed the group mentality and the absence of individualism. In Chengdu there was group exercising all over the city. From 6.15 a.m. onwards, even the old folks' homes spilled out their grey members to dance and stretch together, despite winter darkness. Everywhere, there was group toileting, no privacy, often no doors, just waist high divisions between the holes one squatted over.

Here it was group harvesting. Between three and ten people in a field, or in a contraption sounding like a spluttering lawnmower with steam wafting into the driver's face from the water-cooled engine, and the trailer filled with laughing families or work units and/or produce.

Every inch of available land was cropped; even the earthen walls dividing the fields sprouted leafy greens on top. We saw vertical climbs to impossible harvests. Every town was self-sufficient, with its shops, welders, brick makers and hydro-electric station.

Our under-powered, overloaded bus of veteran design, with speeds of slow and stop, was fined for speeding down the hairpin bends! We spent 45 seconds travelling through a new mountain tunnel; the rest of the five day journey from Chengdu to Dengke by loosely clinging track on the shifting mountainside. The tarmac terminated into drifting dust, which smarted our eyes, clogged our noses and irritated our lungs. Dust masks were issued. We splashed under waterfalls or bumped over rushing streams.

1 p.m. Another traffic jam as landslides blocked the road. Our policeman, Mr Li, tried to sort it out. Three minutes of movement, another stop, thirty metres forward, a pause on the edge of a precipitous cliff. We held our breath, as, swaying from side to side, the bus lurched on another half mile before the next stop. The uneven waltz of the bus and trucks weaving round each other, or round landslides, or avoiding precipices, or the inevitable breakdown, brought the pile of suitcases and rucksacks piled up on the back seat crashing onto the heads and shoulders of the back passengers with painful regularity as we jerked over the rough road to the next obstacle. Dry biscuit and bottled water served as breakfast, lunch and tea. We saw four beehives in front of someone's home at 1100 metres, the same height as Ben Nevis. After skirting another hole in the road, the driver stopped at 2.20 p.m. wanting refreshment, but it was decided to carry on, as the mountain pass was only open to traffic from our end for a few hours a day, and we had a welcome committee waiting for us at the summit of the pass.

3 p.m. We stopped to relieve ourselves amongst the sweetcorn, and walked about to exercise those parts the jolting of the bus had not reached, even with its rigours. Our Chinese speakers enjoyed communicating to the ever-present army personnel amidst much laughter. One word all the Chinese know is 'Hello', accompanied with giggles and shy glances.

3.30 – 4 p.m. Another stop. It was very hot in the full sun. We bathed our limbs in the readily available stream beside the road —so refreshing. At 2700 metres we passed a child and a woman sitting beside the roadway, knitting, perhaps waiting for a bus, we surmised. By 3000 metres, the altitude was telling on some of our team. Rob, Kevin, Madalyn and Wei Shen, pale faced and heavy-headed, stumbled out of the bus into the coolness of the mountain summit, where we all received a welcome from a smiling delegation from Ganzi prefecture. There was a speech of welcome. The wail of brakes announced the cautious descent over some rock-strewn part of the pass. Vehicles proceeded extremely slowly past road gangs with the never ending task of mending and renewing the eroding road, all by hand. Just as coming up the mountain, our engine needed frequent drinks of bottled water to enable it to gasp its way to the top, so now on its descent, the tyres, burning hot with braking, needed buckets of regular refreshment from the roadside stream.

After thirteen hours and thirty-five minutes in the bus, we arrived in Luding hot, hungry and dusty. It was 7.20 p.m. We were greeted by speeches calling us distinguished guests and expressing appreciation for the proposed project of painting the school and hospital, supplying solar powered hot and cold running water to the hospital and for cultural exchange in the field of medicine. Mel responded appropriately and Peter Anderson translated.

We had a colourful meal which I believe included eel. Our rooms were fascinating; the light bulb had melted the lampshade; there was no glass in the door to the balcony; and in order to flush the toilet, one turned on a tap hard above the cistern. Sometimes it worked. It was the best they had and compared to our future living conditions, luxurious.

Breakfast was rice gruel (like a thin porridge), spiced turnip, chips and dumplings. At 9 a.m. we set out on our morning guided tour through the busy market where belts, food, children's clothes and shoes, and half carcasses of pig, elbowed their claim to be sold. Mini tractors with maxi decibels tried to clatter their way through the seething throng of customers; a noticeable number were Tibetans with their distinctive dress and Kumba speech of the district, but most were Chinese, where the fashionable young ladies sported stretch trousers and high heels, their long plaited hair having a quiff stiff with lacquer in front. The river roared through the town and under our feet as we crossed a new bridge. There was no traffic here as the bridge was a good six centimetres higher than the adjoining roads. We visited the monument to the taking of the Luding Bridge during the Long March, then recrossed the tumbling torrent on the swaying chain and plank bridge. Then into a museum commemorating this historic event, and saw two videos of the area and the re-enacting of the battle. Mr Li was obviously thrilled to show us this beautiful area.

After lunch and a stop for petrol (there were no diesel vehicles outside the city), we began the long, slow climb up to Kangding. The buildings changed to stone-based, wooden-planked Tibetan houses. To us, it seemed more attractive to live in the country than in town.

Kangding: the gateway town to the closed area; permits and protocol. Faces and dress were more noticeably Tibetan. The bus stopped at 3.30 p.m. and much to our amazement, we were greeted with an overwhelming chorus of chanting, flower-waving, painted-faced, brightly clad children. The band accompaniment of trumpet, drum and cymbals gave a military touch to match the young players' white and red uniforms. Here we were allocated rooms (three to a room). There were five sinks glassed off from the corridor, locked up at night. There were two squat toilets for each sex per floor, behind a door which almost shut. Huge kettles for the hot water flasks sang on electric rings on each landing, all watched over by the *fuyan*, whose duties kept her up as long as her customers.

After a speech of welcome and Mel's response, we had two hours free to tour the town. We found the post office, where an unhurried assistant took our money for postcards and stamps, flicked her fingers dexterously over an abacus calculator, opened a drawer full of disordered notes and jerked us the change. Paper money predominates, although I did receive a coin in my change in a Chengdu shop, which the restaurant refused to accept. Foreigners are given one type of currency at the banks, to use in most shops, hotels and restaurants in the city and to buy air tickets. However, outside the city and on some street-markets, one has to use the People's Money, which can be changed outside the hotels by the lurking spivs calling to every passing foreigner, "Changey money". The unit of currency is the yuan, often referred to as *quai*, and comes in various colours. The next note down comes in two sizes, two colours and again has two names: the *jaiou* or *maiou*. The tiny 'monopoly money', the *fen*, comes in three values but two colours. The picture on it gives the clue to its worth. The lowest sports a lorry (one driver = one fen), the next an aeroplane (driver and navigator = two fen), and the five fen is symbolised by a ship, which needs captain and crew. These fen are often used to pay the bicycle attendant for parking and, incredibly, finding your bike amongst the shiny ranks of handlebars standing in orderly attention on the edge of every wide pavement in town. The outdated postal service is under review. The dimly lit, dusty wooden interiors of casual calm are being pushed out of the old routine, where the average person receives only five pieces of post per year, into the modern hi-tech world of communication, speed, satellites and fax machines. Junkmail has yet to reach Kangding. Meanwhile, we used the free glue for our stamps and left the green-painted post office, and, passing stalls and shops of socks and sacks of spice, we found the local superstore. Inside it felt empty, not just lacking customers, but articles displayed in the glass cabinets were few and far between. Lighting was frugal; non-existent on the stairs. We peered at the goods; the shop-girls seemed surprised that we actually wanted to look at items and try them on, and even more astonished when Grant wanted to buy the Tibetan hat, Rob the gloves and Sandra the boots. They fairly fluttered in their flurry to fetch out the goods, and whispered in amazement when we paid and smiled. But we were in the part of China where special permits are needed, and for Westerners without a Chinese 'guide', shopping freely is rare.

Three of the team members found a Christian church and had fellowship and prayer with the elder and his wife, who hold three services each Sunday, and baptise the Christians in the hot springs up the mountain.

At 6 p.m. we were treated to a banquet. They had gone to so much trouble. Carved baskets made of watermelon, filled with lychee and other fruit, formed the centrepiece to the revolving glass pivot on each table. We had our first taste of yak —it tasted like beef with aniseed. We walked through the town to a party in a community hall, and were greeted with a clapping welcome. Six tall, majestic Tibetan girls took the hands—and encircled the waists—of six of our younger lady team members, speaking words of greeting in English, and smilingly led the way upstairs to a large hall, where chairs were arranged in small semicircles round low tables groaning with sweets and peanuts and teacups. A set of drums, a keyboard and microphones on the stage seemed out of place as the dancers, wearing age-old costumes, moved with ballet-like grace, their long chiffon sleeves waving like pennants in a breeze. Everyone wore make-up: men, women, boys and girls —

blackened eyes, blushing cheeks, ruby lips. The costumes of the children, and their facial differences, portrayed the various areas and nationalities which make up China. They performed different dance steps in turn, held together with a disco beat. We were invited to share a party piece. We had practised the local favourite, the Kangding Love Song, which we attempted to sing in Chinese, much to our audience's surprise and delight! The Tibetans move their entire bodies when singing. They are full of rhythm and movement, so they loved the actions to our next songs from our Christian culture: *From the rising of the sun* and *If I were a butterfly*. Peter Anderson translated some of the meaning of *Amazing Grace* and *How great thou art*. Then we were invited to join in a circle for their dancing. It looked so easy: a simple stamp and twist of the foot, and a flowing movement of the arms; so graceful, but so very demanding and tiring. The party over, we crunched our way over the empty peanut shells, stumbled down the unlit staircase and enjoyed a lovely stroll back to the hotel. We used an enamel bowl to wash in our bedroom, tried to close the curtains but they did not quite meet on the wire. Seeing the broken window, we decided we needed the fresh air anyway, and slept.

The alarm bleeped us into the dim reality of a new Tibetan day. However, the drivers were already talking loudly down the corridor. We enjoyed our 7 a.m. breakfast of rice gruel and dumplings, waited for the slight dispute over whether there was a television and video in Dengke (for the school presentation) to be sorted out, and climbed aboard the dust-shrouded bus. Chris and John decided to join the film crew in the land cruiser as sphincter muscle controls were not assured. We inched our way out of Kangding, creeping down the narrow lanes, jerking across the bridge over the clamorous river and out into the clear bright countryside.

Five public buses overtook our sober to slow progress, each crammed full of people and luggage: chickens clucked in open-work baskets on the roof. We climbed unsteadily, swerving round small rocks scattered over the road. We surmised that these had been used as chocks to stop the broken-down vehicles from rolling downhill. Never trust in brakes! We were to learn from our own experience as we spluttered to a stop at over 4000 metres. The thin air did not mix correctly with the fuel, causing the engine to cough and wheeze. Applying the brakes sharply caused the air pump to fail, so out we climbed to enjoy the scene. Madalyn felt decidedly wobbly with the altitude. Arne recommended drinking lots of bottled water.

We saw our first nomadic tent, its black yak hairwoven fabric smoking with the prospect of food cooking over mud stoves. Any bugs daring to venture inside were immediately kippered into harmlessness. Three children driving sheep before them came from the tent towards us, running straight uphill, passing at a respectful distance below us. We waved. One girl came back close enough to study us carefully, a solitary sentinel in far flung places. She was offered an egg, but refused. She seemed to want to be friendly but could not understand us. She leapt lightly down the scree like a mountain goat to the tent, setting off the bush radio.

We had time to observe the beautiful flowers of gentian blue, yellow pom-poms, white edelweiss and deep pink, spiky, saucer-like stemless marvels that few people ever see or appreciate, blooming in the grass because it is God's pleasure to give them the nature to bloom where he places them. What a lesson for us humans, so squeezed into the mould of performing our best for others' opinions, rather than living out God's nature in us wherever we are planted.

Although the air was only half the pressure we were used to, we tried singing *Make Way*, *Meekness and Majesty* and *Shine Jesus, Shine*. Gareth and Mel provided accompaniment, percussion rendered by hands banging on seat backs, setting the dust flying afresh.

The girl climbed back up from the tent over the hilltop behind us, caught up with the other two, and when we wound round the mountain, after a one and a half hour repair stop, we saw the trio skipping nimbly down the other side, trying to head off the sheep from running into the path of our bus. Although most of the hillsides produced only rough grass, many small bushes grew right to the top and there is evidence of many trees having been sawn down, leaving just the stumps. Log lorries were the most common sight. A Tibetan boy with a sling in his hand, about to round up or encourage onwards some yak, goat and sheep, performed his work for the day. Around us we saw many terraces abandoned and beginning to fall into disrepair. Perhaps this area had been more populated years ago. The Tibetans preferred to farm the valley floor. We passed logs floating down the rivers, many marooned on shallows. Great compounds housed the woodworkers' units, armed not with chainsaws, but large hand saws.

We lurched languidly over the hard-packed rocks, wrapped in a cosy layer of dust, which nested in our ears and on our eyelashes. The next obstacle was roadworks; not the traffic light, orange coned, orderly variety common here, but a complete take-over by a gang of men shovelling and scooping, cementing and improving. The blockage diverted our reeling bus through three hundred metres of ruts and quagmire. Alighting, we balanced from one stone to another through the boggy wasteland churned up by heavy lorries.

Climbing aboard, we realised how we were being taught patience and how unnecessary it was to be too ambitious in keeping to time limits. Our lunch stop was at 6.30 p.m. Meanwhile, we passed over a wide, cultivated valley where horses grazed and the omnifunctional yak, yoked in pairs, ploughed land already harvested. This amazing animal provides hair for rope and weaving, strength for farming, dung for fuel, a means of transporting people and cargo, skins for winter-wearing, meat for food, mild butter and the most delicious yoghurt, which became our breakfast favourite. The Tibetans, their leisurely leathered faces so brown that the cheeks were almost purple, carted huge loads on their broad backs.

For the first time in China, we saw a tractor and a combine harvester ready to work on bigger fields of lush barley, corn, cabbages and onions. This rich, fertile, well-watered valley was mostly worked by hand. We could have been in the Lake District or the Scottish Highlands on a sunny day, except for the presence of prayer flags of Buddhist temples. We passed through a large, colourful village. Horses stood tethered. Bright rolls of cloth draped the roadside. Local women wore long black dresses, pink blouses; hair decorated with turquoise, gold and coral. As we climbed out of the valley, the drivers kept the sluggish engine moving with another bottle of mineral water, topped up with tea from an old jam jar. We reached Daofu with headaches, and relieved ourselves at the 'conveniences', which smelled like a cattle shed about to be raked out. One straddled over an oblong cut in a wooden board atop a large, dung filled pit.

We left at 7.15 p.m. for another seventy kilometres of bumps and twists and one more traffic jam in the dark, before reaching Luhuo. The hostel was well-built and beautifully painted, with the entrance decorated Tibetan-style. Apparently, it was recently rebuilt after an earthquake in this region.

September 7 We were up at 6.30 a.m., packed the bus and had breakfast before the 8 a.m. start. The new houses going up were excellent. The stone base a metre or so above the ground was topped by substantial, planed, split logs; almost a Swiss chalet look-a-like, with the snow-covered mountains and glaciers gleaming in the crystal clear air. The journey was telling on more of the team. Xu Xin (Sunshine) was very sick on the bus. Many were suffering headaches, diarrhoea and allergies set off by so much dust. We drove to Ganzi, an amazing town built on a hillside topped by a temple. We climbed to the top. It was a gruelling, almost vertical climb of at least a hundred steps after an already stiff clamber up through the town and over the streams. We saw young people with cataracts on their eyes. The view from the top was superb, the monks most hospitable, with tea and biscuits; the buildings were dark and oppressive. On the descent everyone was friendly. A little girl of three came to hold our hands and chat. Some of our team saw a solar cooker parabola in front of someone's house and went to investigate. The Tibetans' smiles have an extra sparkle as they love adding gold crowns to their teeth —a safe place to keep their savings; we did not see a bank. As we left Ganzi behind, we noticed the harvest being stored on the flat roofs like vast brown-yellow thatch. The ploughing was done by one man with two yaks pulling one blade. We reached Maniganggo at 7 p.m. A bleak, Spartan spot. Some could not sleep because of the altitude, the headaches, the cold, or the Tibetan dogs barking fiercely through the night. The compound was laid out in a square around the courtyard where the lorries, landcruiser and bus parked overnight. It was a two hundred yard stroll or sprint, depending on one's gut reaction to the culinary combinations, from the sleeping quarters to the loo pit, and another fifty yards to the washroom. One could perform one's ablutions and have a steady jog at the same time.

September 8 Stars twinkled in the clear dawn. The crystal light revealed the sunlit, snow-capped peak of a glacier which fed the Green Dragon Lake some fifteen miles away. We were to visit this breathtakingly beautiful spot on our return journey. But now it was breakfast: hot, spiced milk; rice gruel, peanuts, cabbage and dumplings. The mist descended as we climbed slowly away from the compound. The road levelled out and we glimpsed enormous herds of yak being driven by their owners, some walking, others riding horses. One man even rode

63

a bicycle; all were carrying their possessions: tents, pots and pans, and boxes. The mist gave the impression of a stampede of stock and a mêlée of migrating nomads. The sun shone through by the seventh group passing by, and we gasped at the rolling grasslands edged with mountains topped by a brilliant blue sky. We passed five men on horseback. These were travelling monks of obvious importance. One of them was a lama, with fine robes of yellow and red, a neat hat and sunglasses. We could see evidence of abandoned tent sites, not litter; we saw none on our journey, just remains of mud stoves, either to be taken up by another family of tent dwellers, or else to disintegrate through rain and frost into the surrounding soil. We stretched our legs on the plateau of grasslands, where wonderful wild flowers dwarfed the minute black frogs. Within minutes, a Tibetan boy appeared, mingling happily with us, catching frogs in his hands, laughing and asking for empty mineral water bottles. We sadly said goodbye to this endless meadow of verdure and beauty, and climbed aboard up another mountain pass. The top measured 4400 metres on the altimeter, the pressure 587 millibars, about half the air we were used to at sea level. It was at the top of this pass that the hovercraft team had to dig its way out of the snow two and a half years ago. We drank in the exquisite beauty and the tricky hairpin bends. The bus needed refreshment, as water boils at 85°C at this height.

It was photo time. Prayer flags and a cairn marked the top of the pass. The only house over the pass was a roadworker's compound. In two hours of further travelling we saw only tents, a buzzard sitting on a post, several swallow-type birds sitting on wires (looking as if they were about to migrate), and over the mountains eagles wheeled regally. At 10.45 a.m. we passed through a small settlement of abandoned mud-built houses. In three hours we had seen only two other vehicles. The road from Maniganggo to Xining had a T-junction to the left at right angles. We turned, and knew immediately that we had left the main road. A large, white tent more like a marquee was situated nearby. Perhaps it was a wedding celebration, we surmised. A separate tent for cooking stood nearby. Outside were five landcruisers, one of which was ours; and we duly pulled off the road into the meadow and parked. What a welcome! We were now fifty miles from our destination, and here was a foretaste of the royal treatment we experienced along the route. All the officials from the county stood in line to shake hands in greeting. Inside the marquee we sat round the walls and were served Tibetan tea, beer, cake, yak joints and spicy dishes, finished by the most delicious thick, creamy, yak yoghurt. Stately Tibetan women served us with quiet dignity. We were told when we left, to expect a welcome from the villagers we passed. It seemed a very empty landscape. Wide, cornflower-blue skies arched above the grasslands. The absence of pollution enabled us to see for many miles in all directions. We jerked over the many streams. At one place a new bridge was in the process of being built over a gully, but it was not connected to the road, so we disembarked and stepped our way across on the stones, while our bus slithered down one bank, bending the chassis, wallowed across the swirling liquid and endeavoured to clamber up the opposite bank. Several Tibetan children swarmed round us, unashamed to ask for the empty water bottles, which they grabbed gleefully. Obstacles now were not broken down lorries but yak and goats, who refused to budge off the track until the last minute and then leapt surefootedly up or down the adjoining mountainside.

We approached a small village, Lanu Gen Leng, at 4 p.m. Everyone was out waving, wearing their best clothes. We realised they had given up their harvesting to wait in the broiling sun for us to pass by. As we walked through, shaking hands and smiling, we were welcomed by musical instruments being played: trumpets and gongs. Some young boy monks lifted high a large framed photo of a lama. Men, flashing gold teeth as they grinned, stood holding colourfully-decorated horses draped in tinkling bells. Children waved flowers, chanting, "Welcome, foreigner!"

We climbed back aboard the bus. The two seats behind the driver were now being held up by wooden logs, as all the bumping and lurching had sent the seat supports through the floor. Half an hour of jerks, jars and jolts brought us to Maga, where the villagers gave us an ecstatic welcome usually reserved for film stars. Horse-riders pursued us to the next stop. The crumbling, precipitous road afforded us, at 5.30 p.m., our first view of the Yangtze snaking towards the horizon. Cameras clicked through the bus window.

Changtou, our last stop before our destination, had been sizzling all afternoon, waiting patiently for us. Tibetans really do work on flexi time, as we were to experience over the next two weeks. Here, we were greeted with a welcome of more trumpets and chanting and a most

65

amazing cavalcade of some fifty horsemen, who followed the bus like a posse from a cowboy film. They soon overtook us, either to show off their skills of horsemanship, or to avoid the choking dust the bus threw up. They arrived in Dengke before us. We crossed a bridge and got out of the bus. The whole town was lining the streets. Men and women danced and sang, children chanted, everyone smiled, some happy to shake hands, others too shy. What a crowd! They said, "Hello", and we replied *"Demo"*. After a quarter of a mile, we walked through the gates of the hostel compound and were given our rooms. We were housed up two flights of steps and our room had two wooden beds, a table, a washing line, three enamel washing bowls, an electric bulb, which fluctuated from fifteen to forty five watts when there was not a daily power cut, and almost wall-to-wall floors. There was a cosy opening where wall and floor had become detached over time, through which our friendly rat used to visit us nightly and play diverting games like tossing a cup into the centre of the room. After some nights of attempting to deflect our interesting neighbour by wedging bags and socks into the gaps, we turned for help to our hosts, who promptly broke beer bottles and cemented the jagged fragments around the skirting, thus deterring further exploits. Discouraged from his evening romps in our chamber, our rat transferred to Reidun's, to scare the three nurses sharing a room by sharing their cheese from the compo rations.

The ablutions were quite a walk away out of the building, down the steps, over a stream and into an open barn, where a man fed a large stove with wood to boil the water, brought by handcart, in a thirty gallon oil drum, from the river at the top of the village. It looked like an enormous, old-fashioned copper. A similar metal dish was next to it, filled with cold water, and a large ladle enabled us to fill our bowls with the required amount. A trestle and bench were nearby, on which to rest one's bowl, or one could bathe *al fresco* by carrying the bowl to the steps over the stream, or to logs piled outside. They had built a large coffin-shaped bath in an adjoining room, with a wooden wedge as a plug. One stood in it and poured water from the bowl. Dengke had no taps, plumbing nor drains, so dirty water was tossed onto the soil to drain naturally. However, after several days of rain, the bathroom turned into a quagmire. The pigs enjoyed it! The lavatories next door to the barn had recently been whitewashed on the outside, and 'ladies' and 'gentlemen' were written in Chinese and English. The pit had been cleared. They had gone to enormous effort to make us feel welcome. The men's side had a dim electric bulb, whose rays crept through the loose panelling into the ladies' five stalls. We shared a common pit. Privacy was virtually non-existent. One night, when at one's most vulnerable, squatting over the missing plank, nether clothing around the shins, it was very disconcerting to hear the sniffling of an animal entering the doorless arch. Was it a pig or a goat? I came face to face with a soulless dog, full of mange and mud and menace. I swallowed hard and prayed. "Good dog," I remarked unconvincingly. After a few sniffs, he shuffled off uninterestedly. Tension eased.

At the first evening meal, we heard speeches of welcome and toasts to our visit. Then our local dignitaries sang. Apparently, as much as the Chinese make speeches, the Tibetans sing. As they sing they sway, rhythm oozing from all pores, and everyone claps in time. It became a skill to sit on the fifteen centimetre wide trestles for over an hour. Sometimes a colourful Tibetan rug will be thrown over a bench (never on the floor), but not once did I see a cushion. What a hardy race they are, and how soft we are.

September 9 6 a.m. We woke with a start. Whatever was that noise? It could not be low-flying aeroplanes or intercity trains. We discovered it was Radio China at full pitch (that never was quite tuned into the station). A loudspeaker was cunningly positioned on a tree, not far from the hostel and in other parts of Dengke, so on cue, everyone is woken up by news and views. It reminded one of holiday camp loud-speaker systems jerking the campers into holiday mood. Dogs had barked through the night. We had two large sheds with locks, in which to store the paints, pumps, panels, pipes, penicillin, portaloo, paper, pens and pultruded plastic parts —in fact, all the properties ready for the project. Engineering items, boxes and necessities went in one shed, and medicine, compo rations and educational material in the other, along with the stiff brushes for the daily sweep around the top boards of the loo pit. The water purifying unit was set up in the wash house. With everything stored and stacked, we washed ready for lunch. The procession of waitresses carrying each dish from the cooking house a hundred metres up the lane around the hostel, to a dining hall another hundred metres away reminded me of a medieval banquet, with the long trek from the kitchens to the great hall. At 3500 metres, we were not too bothered by flies and wasps. Although the food was never hot, it was very colourful and varied. They went to enormous expense providing us with delicacies, but they soon got the hint that ducks' feet and beak were not top of our pop-it-in-the-mouth list! So we settled eventually for cabbage soup, bean curd, yak strips and lots of rice. However, with the Dengke trots taking their grip, or gripe, more turned to comfort food to be found in the compo rations, like fruit salad, cheese, corned beef, chicken curry and Weetabix, all very out of date, having been given to the hovercraft expedition two and a half years ago. At 2 p.m. we sallied forth to view our potential work sites. Down the street, past the green painted post office (that opened when the carpenter boss had finished his task for the day, so I saw it open only once), round the corner, past the horses tethered under the trees, and in through the gates of the school compound. The ground was baked earth: two basketball nets denoted the only sports facility in the town. A class of fourteen year-olds was practising marching and drill, not something in our National Curriculum. The school buildings were set out on three sides of a muddy courtyard, which after five days of rain, later in our stay, became a quagmire, where the pigs wallowed contentedly. We had planned to paint the school with special ICI Weathershield paint, which could withstand the incredible range in temperature, but when the Chinese officials saw it, they said they were going to pull it down and build another. We were not surprised; even a coat of paint could not hide the missing glass in the windows, or the window frame nailed in place by cross beams.

Children sat in their classes: maths, chemistry, and pronunciation, mostly learning by rote. Facilities were minimal. Most children have schooling until age nine and then some stay on for the middle school. Here in Dengke, they work a shift system to accommodate the three hundred being educated. There is no other school for many miles, so children come from neighbouring villages to board with relations or friends and then walk home at the weekend. But if you live too far, or know no one to care for your children, then they go unschooled. Part of the idea of giving tapes to the headmaster was to record lessons for the nomad families, many of whom own battery-driven hi-fi systems, and for others who fall outside the education bracket.

At the end of one classroom, on the outside wall, was a beautiful picture of welcome and friendship, drawn in coloured chalks. Artistry flowed from the Tibetans. We retraced our steps and climbed the hill towards the hospital. It was fiercely hot, yet we did not sweat. The brilliance of the light hurt our eyes. No wonder local people wore hats: the men a high, crown-brimmed felt hat, usually in cream; the women, in this district at least, with a bright brocade covered stiffened device, like a partly opened fan, held down on the top of their head by their plaits which were looped around it. It was an ingenious sunshade for face and neck.

As we crossed the stream, we noticed a little girl waiting in her best Tibetan gown. Someone remarked that she looked like the picture on the Project Dengke shirt many were wearing. Udren had befriended Rob during the last team visit, where they had used as Base Camp 1 a grassy meadow by the river Yangtze near Tub (Wen Tuo), the next village upstream from Dengke. She and her friends had spent hours watching and helping these European strangers as they drove the two hovercraft up and down stream, and as the doctors treated any sick who came for help. Rob had shown her an old photo of our four children, and she had sped home and brought a rubber ball as a gift for the youngest. It was probably her only toy, and it was accepted as if it were gold. Bringing it down to sea level caused it to collapse under the air pressure, but it remains a treasured possession, a symbol of the kindliness of these hardy folk. Here she stood, pointing at Rob, who remembered her with ragged hair and clothes, and was nonplussed by this brushed and spruced version two and a half years bigger! She had heard of our coming, and had walked from her village with an aunt and, now holding hands, came with us to find the hospital, beaming with smiles, calling us 'abba' and 'amma' (daddy and mummy). Her own father had died before the last expedition and we learnt her little sister had gone too.

Through the hospital gates we gazed at a newly whitewashed building, the paint tub still outside —so much for our offer of help. However, the inside needed doing and we walked round to assess the best place for positioning the pump shed, the route of the trench to be dug, bringing water from the stream above the weir to the hospital, where hot and cold water would be on tap. Village children, pigs and dogs followed us freely. Everyone was in relaxed mode, tension was minimal, urgency nominal, hurry non-existent. Doctors sat drinking tea and laughing, grownups cracked peanuts dexterously between the gleaming white and the glistening gold of their teeth. Pigs rooted round outside and in; we even saw one doctor drive through the corridors on his motorbike! It was not a place where we fancied having surgery, but what could beat the relaxed bedside manner, and the restful recuperation to be enjoyed here? All the villagers wanted to help. But first we had to draw up a strategic list of who was doing what, at the team meeting later that evening.

The two heavy, waterproof boxes encasing the satellite phone and tracking system were set up successfully and we had contact home, thanks to Starcom UK Ltd., based in Gorleston, Norfolk.

September 10 The meeting room was upstairs, at the end of the corridor. Tibetan rugs draped the seats edging the room just big enough to sit our thirty-member team. Metal tables in the centre had electric rings incorporated, where large kettles filled our tea cups and flasks. The wiring was original, yet complex, as it wormed its way from the tables across the wooden floor and crawled up the wall. This was the cleaning ladies' dormitory. They needed no wardrobes. They slept in what they wore daily; the coat is never abandoned. If it is warm, they shed one sleeve (which is how the dancers dress). If it is hot, both sleeves are tied round the waist. Only the face and hands are ever uncovered, burnt by the stealthy sun's intrusive rays; their rosy cheeks purpled by exposure to stiff wind, stinging dust storms, sub-zero frosts and sizzling sun.

We met at 8 a.m. for devotions, breakfasted at 8.30, and reloaded the lorry with equipment for the hospital at 9 a.m. Meanwhile, the doctors, Arne Brantsaeter, Kevin Ilsley, Lim Wei Shen and Gareth Clegg, had already gone up to the hospital with Janet Baaijens, Barbara Forbes and Reidun Haugen the nurses, and Val Thomson the physiotherapist, to discuss the role and possible objectives of the medical team. Dr Jon Martin was getting no better since our arrival, and during the day he developed pneumonia. After a nightmare journey for him, he was now invalided out, needing rest and a loving wife's ministrations of compo food and cuddles. Val and Barbara were interested in looking at leprosy rehabilitation. The hospital had records of seven lepers in the area, all successfully treated, and the disease halted; although they all still lived as outcasts in society. Methods of coaxing disabled hands into some movement, by rubbing with Vaseline etc., were to be tried. Reidun was interested in looking at the health care system in general, having written a book herself for the Norwegian

Health Service, used as a textbook in the training of nurses. Arne hoped to do a bacteriological survey of the water, in context, with the engineering programme.

They were given a tour of the hospital and briefly documented the four very sick patients being treated, always aware of the need for sensitivity. Three of the four were being given the same palliative care (rest and medicine) as we practise. They could foresee a problem that local people would come to the hostel for medical help instead of the hospital, thinking Western medicine would always succeed where Tibetan and Chinese had failed. Firstly, this would be unfair to our hosts; secondly, it would be unfair to the team and thirdly, although pharmaceutical companies had been generous in supplying basic medicines, we did have limited resources. It was agreed to work in co-operation with the hospital, at all times. Kevin, the doctor in charge, felt time was short and that we were here to learn as well as teach, and we needed to get involved in looking at Chinese medicinal practices. Our doctors were keen to be available for joint clinics, anytime. Leprosy clinic was fixed for the 14th so that rehabilitation practices could be compared.

Medicine had been brought as a gift. Chengdu was 1000 kilometres away and, as we had experienced, transport was difficult so receiving up to date equipment and drugs was a problem. Kevin was happy to organise a seminar to explain how our structures work. The staff at the hospital consisted of two graduates from Chengdu, one who had been in Dengke for thirty years, a Chinese medicine expert, a Tibetan medicine expert, a radiologist, a leprosy expert and a technician. One of the patients was awaiting an appendix operation.

Rob Watson, Mel Richardson and John Whatmore, members of the previous expedition, Peter Coulson, Barbara and Sandra, with some of the Chinese drivers and interpreters, set off for Udren's village, a roller-coaster ride three kilometres away. She was waiting with her friends at the base of the village, set on a hill, approached by a zig zag path. We gasped our way to the top, through a maze of narrow alleys, to a large white tent set up outside her home. Mel wanted to find the old goatherd he had become acquainted with two and a half years ago. Just then, he passed by in the distance. Udren pointed at him walking along the road. The children skipped off after him to bring him into the tent, where he was given a seat of honour. All the village crowded round to watch. We gave Udren some bubbles, balloons, pens, a

T-shirt, with her face grinning happily, and a Polaroid photo. She gave us a silk khata (scarf) and bowls of yak milk and sweets. The humble mother's wrinkled face, furrowed by suffering and sun, folded into gentle smiles of welcome. We could not guess her age.

The men walked down to the site of Base Camp 1. The villagers had cleared the stones from the riverside to make a runway for the hovercraft two and a half years ago and it was still uncovered. There were moving memories for Mel, John and Rob. Barbara and Sandra came down another route and discovered the local leper lady sitting under a tree. We felt we were back in Bible times and as disciples of Jesus, the lepers' friend, we greeted her. Barbara spoke some words in Tibetan. Her rheumy eyes gazed appealingly at us, and we put our hands on her shoulders for a prayer before joining the others.

At the hospital, the solar water pump was being set up, the solar cooker prototype trial was fixed up and walls started to be washed and rendered with some of the cement we had brought. Lucy's modular pultruded plastic building blocks from Maunsell Structural Plastics Ltd were being washed and stacked, ready to be made into a shelter for the pump and tanks.

Reidun and Barbara finished the afternoon by walking up the mountain behind Dengke, talking to the women there. Reidun was offered, and accepted, a ride on a Tibetan horse up and down the road —her first time on horseback.

John phoned the Chengdu police to see how investigations were going concerning his money belt left behind in a wayside loo the first day out on our journey. He had reasoned with himself that to fret and worry about it would be of no use, so had seen the local police and left the matter with them. Everything was found intact and great was his rejoicing! It was 10.15 a.m., and he decided to ring his wife, Christine, to tell her the good news —not that she even knew the bad news! Her sleepy voice reminded him of the time difference. It was 3.15 a.m. in England, but she made all the right noises to his enthusiasm!

For the second evening running, we noticed that after our supper a coloured ball of light had been revolving in the dining room, while the Chinese danced a very neat formal waltz and a disco choreography of exquisite footwork. We learnt that we were invited the next day to join them in a party to celebrate the autumn festival.

September 11 After breakfast and loo scrub, it was time for school.

Tables and benches were set out in the playground with sweets, tea and apples. When the hovercraft team visited the school two and a half years ago, some pictures of aspects of English life and its importance to 7–11 year old children, from Orford Church of England Voluntary Aided Primary School, had been given to the school. What the Dengke students made of Garfield and Snoopy and roller skates etc., I do not know; but some of their pictures came back of Tibetan life —carefully drawn horses in their finery, ladies in best dresses, and carvings and decorations on houses. The Orford children would admit that the Tibetan children had done much better drawings, even though the paper was tissue thin and colours limited. We took photos of some of the Dengke artists. Mel, Colin, Gareth and Grant entertained the waiting folk to Christian songs. They crowded around the guitar-playing quartet, grinning with simple joy. We took our places and Xu Xin (Sunshine) distributed straw hats as the sun was already blazing down.

Ten men in heavy boots, baggy trousers, fur hats and coats with one sleeve on and one off were joined by ten long-sleeved, pink-bloused and coated ladies, each with at least twenty long plaits. (The belt is a most important item of clothing. The plaits are tucked in it, and con- tained. From the belt hang down knives, purses, chains; or a dagger in the men's case, and little scarves with tasselled ends.) The simple steps looked masculine on the energetic men, and feminine on the modestly bowed women. As they danced, they sang loudly. Children danced next, with multi-coloured striped pinafores. More adults danced, the men swirling and diving in their vigorous movements; a drum beat accompanied them. A brother and sister sang. Sichuan TV videoed the entertainment. Then it was our turn to sing the *Kangding Love Song*; *From the Rising of the Sun* and *Guide me, O thou Great Jehovah*. The area Chief then sang a song, followed by more dancing. Udren was invited to sing but she was too shy, so a man from her village did the honours. What a morning, what these people lack in tarmac and taps they certainly gain in colour and culture.

After lunch, at which Udren appeared, we all walked to the out- skirts of the town, where a large marble plaque, engraved with the words 'China—UK. Friendship Monument', and weighing a tonne, was cemented on a roadside boulder as a reminder to all coming into town. There were speeches and photos and then a walk halfway back to the town, where we planted a token branch each (thirty trees will be planted in the winter), which will become a picnic site near the river. Here we met one of Udren's two big brothers. However, up the valley, visibility began to dim, and before we could all reach the hostel, the blistering day of sunshine turned into a stinging dust storm, the wind bending the trees double; and this was followed by a mighty thunderstorm with lashing rain. By 6 p.m. we were back from the valley of the shadow to still waters and green pastures.

By the evening, Jon's pneumonia was no better and Rob was feeling very feverish. He, too, was diagnosed as having pneumonia. Later that evening, Janet the nurse joined the others on a bed of sickness. All three had come to China straight from busy jobs; Janet already weak from a sickness picked up in Nepal. The sheer stamina called on to survive the journey, coupled with the altitude and change of diet, meant that they were feeling low and therefore more open to infection. Our doctors were busy handing out antibiotics, and Val, the physiotherapist, filled her hours squeezing and pummelling lungs to bring up the phlegm.

Meanwhile, Geralyn and Sandra made some posters of Jesus saying, "I am the good shepherd." These were to be given out at the school presentation the next day, Saturday 12th. The shepherd was depicted as wearing Tibetan-style clothing. After making several pictures each, we gave everyone in the team three blank pages on which to copy from the examples, so that over a hundred were ready in time. Even Mr Li, the policeman, joined in. How convenient photocopying is!

8 p.m. The party began, with very sweet nuts, apples and drinks provided. The room was filled with folk from the town —Tibetan and Chinese, as well as team members. Mel was leading the entertainment with his karaoke machine. Then there was an attempt to integrate. Much to our surprise, it is usual for women to dance together and men to dance together. Mr Li, the policeman, asked Mel for the pleasure. The Chinese danced their quicksteps and waltzes with serious precision. The Tibetans watched.

September 12 Those who were fit to work were forced into wakefulness by the intrusive newsreader outside the window. Today, the projects continued uninterrupted. One of the aims for coming to Dengke was to test renewable energy in such a context.

Nicky Shaw-Hamilton had designed a prototype solar cooker to test at high altitude. Peter Gunner had already set up a water purifier in our wash room, and now he was setting up the tank and taps inside the hospital. Colin Garner was in charge of setting up the water pump. He was thoroughly enjoying his third time in China and loved the hard-working, warm, genuine Tibetans, who were only too pleased to help dig or carry, without being asked. Before digging the trench and laying the pipes, he wanted to make sure the pump would work this high, so connected it up to the generator we had brought and was delighted to learn that it could pump water up to the hospital over 200 metres away. Peter Kofoed, a student from Copenhagen who earned himself the title of the 'Great Dane', provided brain as well as brawn in the engineering field. Mike Wisheart, helped by Paul Glendenning (doing New Material Exposure Trials), was in charge of the solar water heating system. Solar panels were to be erected on the pultruded plastic building, the erection of which was overseen by civil engineer Lucy Maunsell, who would evaluate its construction and usage. These panels would provide energy to both move and heat the water. Grant Freeman from Powergen Management donned a boilersuit and became an electrician again, helped by Rob, to rewire the hospital —a dangerous job involving getting lost in the loft; but also very rewarding, as he built up a good relationship with the local Chinese electrical boss, very keen to learn his techniques. They also brought electric light into the kindergarten classroom; a tricky job, as nailing the wire from the power source in the school teacher's house on the rotten bargeboards overhead proved frustrating and challenging.

Madalyn Brooks, chief painter and decorator, used her personnel management skills in sorting out plans and accomplishing of action, helped by Peter and Geralyn Anderson, when they were not using their talents as interpreters, and Hazel Gunner, who doubled up in the engineering field to help her father, Peter; also, Christine Martin and Sandra Watson, the nurses/doctors, when not busy elsewhere, two delightful Chinese ladies in their twenties, 'Sunshine' from Chengdu Foreign Affairs Office and Lily, the interpreter with the last expedition, who had just completed a year's course in English at Loughborough College, staying with Mel Richardson's family, and like a daughter to them. Mel and John Whatmore did some painting when other duties allowed. John and Peter Coulson had a tight schedule filming each aspect of the work to make into a documentary. Andrew Sneller, an estate agent, put his skills to work surveying and charting the buildings and environs of Dengke. Sam Brooks from ICI was foreman directing willing volunteers toward tasks for the day, and logging the data collected from the various tests onto a computer. It was an excellent team; everyone was needed. Washing and painting walls in the hospital complex meant three and a half rooms were finished by the end of the day. The medics had a joint surgery, which went well. They talked about leprosy treatment. The Chinese/Tibetans were aiming at a policy by the year 2000, and wanted collaboration with other nationalities. Their chief medic said he was overwhelmed by what was happening in the hospital, medically and electrically. All the main connections have been done in the loft, and Nicky had been up and fixed the split chimney blackening everything in the loft with the smoke. We all wore dustmasks to work there. The Dengke doctors were doing a very good job with their limited resources. No X-rays could be taken, the ultrasound unit did not work and the scanner needed a man from Kangding to repair it. However, with a combination of Western, Tibetan and Chinese medicine, much was being done: an eye complaint was being treated by traditional medicine; a sore throat needed a prescription for antibiotics. However there were no resources to do convert squint and cataract problems.

Barbara and Val went to visit the sick in Udren's village. They found a man of forty nine who needed a doctor urgently; others needing help were encouraged to come to the hospital.

The route of the trench for pipe laying was determined, and the Tibetans watching eagerly offered to dig and carry and clear up. Even the local doctors pitched in, still wearing their white coats and hats.

A presentation had been organised at the school in the afternoon by Mel, John, Peter, Arne, Hazel, Geralyn and Sandra. One of our objectives in Project Dengke was to promote peace, goodwill and understanding using a programme of cultural exchange and friendship projects between the UK and the People's Republic of China. The room was crammed to overflowing with noisy, jostling, excited schoolchildren in best clothes; adults leant through the window. John started with a video and slide presentation of the last expedition. They watched the visuals intently, sometimes seeing themselves. Arne translated into Chinese (all education is done in Chinese here) as Mel went on to speak and give them pictures drawn by Loughborough children. Hazel, our youngest team member, who celebrated her 18th birthday in Dengke, then offered to answer questions about school life in England, Geralyn interpreting.

We realised that children in China are not encouraged to ask questions, but gradually she was asked what she thought of China. "Hot and friendly," she replied. "Is your school beautiful?" was another query. How could she compare it to this one? Then Sandra, a part-time teacher from Orford, Suffolk, showed a tape of her school and the village surroundings and presented gifts from the Orford children —of pictures, jigsaws, a sweatshirt for the headmaster with Orford Castle on it; and from Suffolk County Council paper, plastic folders and pencils. Exxon gave balloons and pens; others had tapes for the school work among the nomads; and each child was given the drawn poster of 'I am the good shepherd', to colour and keep. Afterwards, we enjoyed talking to the headmistress about education, and how in the UK parents are encouraged to be involved on a voluntary basis with reading and raising funds etc., in their children's schools. We gave her the prospectus of a Suffolk high school, and other information about teaching in Suffolk. We wondered if there could be a possibility of a teacher swap in the future. The staff were so gracious and gave us a red banner signifying friendship.

Our three members with pneumonia were now suffering side effects from the antibiotics and needed anti-diarrhoea medication; Rob recovering, Jon worse, Janet very weak. There was a queue at the satellite phone for home calls. It seemed amazing that within seconds we were linked with loved ones, assuring them of safe arrival and goals being reached. The team meeting at 8 p.m. had a buoyant atmosphere and prayers were led by Sam and Madalyn. Barbara joined the ranks of the 'Dengke trotters', but her anti-diarrhoea tablet gave her a reaction which, without the immediate, vigilant care of our doctors, would have proved fatal. It took several hours of prayer and ministrations before she was over the worst. We breathed again.

September 13 Sunday. Hallelujah! The Christians' special day of rejoicing at Christ's resurrection and grace was not disturbed by Radio China until 10 a.m. After breakfast at 8.30, we had an hour of fellowship and praise. A local village had helped the team of the stricken hovercraft expedition after an accident involving rapids and rocks, two and a half years ago, and a visit was planned to Ren Ko Xi via bus and horseback for the present team. After a bus ride of an hour we were met by gaily decorated horses draped in bells and carpets, and grinning Tibetan owners, who eventually saw us all mounted, and we set off downhill through two villages of waving people. After half an hour, most of us, unused to horse riding, were happy to dismount, as the uneven track was too steep and the rocks too loose for safety. We zig zagged down, remounted, some of us looking far too big on such small horses, and crossed a very fast flowing stream. It took one and a half hours to reach our destination. It was from here the eight hovercraft team members had hired horses to make the five hour journey back to base camp —on mountain tracks, with horrendous drops to the Yangtze below. We received another warm Tibetan welcome, with clapping and khatas, and were taken to the chief's beautiful house, to eat yoghurt, with a buttery, nutty tasting barley compound (eaten with fingers), and boiled water to wash it down. Most of the house was filled with harvest; our upstairs dining room had one wall opening out on the courtyard below. Villagers swarmed about at a discreet distance.

We followed a track down to the river to see the sight of the accident, and were overtaken by a short but dramatic thunderstorm. Back at the village, we were directed to our 'rent-a-rides' and, before we had gone far, an icy rain drove into our faces. The Tibetans followed us. None had waterproofs as we know them, but they were certainly hardy. It was warming to dismount and climb up the steep track that had turned to mud and mire. Our sure-footed beasts brought us back through the villages, where folk stood in the sheeting downpour to wish us well.

The sight of out decrepit bus meant comfort and warmth to our chilled limbs. The Great Dane was sure he would freeze to death! Sam had managed to inflame a hip joint, his long legs cramped to impossible angles astride his mount. Back at the hostel we dived into dry clothes and sleeping bags to defrost. After a good meal, patients were visited and a precious bar of chocolate shared around.

September 14 Dogs barked most of the night, and rats were also busy scurrying. Earplugs were a great help, especially at the 6 a.m. radio reveille. The weather had followed an exact pattern the last four days —a dry hot morning until 3 p.m., then a storm force wind bringing thunderstorms and rain for one and a half hours. The electricity cut out each day; and another pane or two of glass broke in the hostel. There were no refuse collectors. Everything got thrown out of a certain window between the two flights of stairs. What did the locals do with their rubbish? Tissues and nappies are non-existent, although pine toilet paper is a prerequisite on every table at every meal, to wipe out the bowls and rub the chopsticks! Many of us just dipped them in our tea (the hot water killed most of the nasties lurking.) Five of the seven rooms were now finished at the hospital. What a difference! Rewiring was going well, and the trench for the pipes was almost finished. The nurses held their leprosy clinic and saw seven lepers discussing their rehabilitation with our hosts. The doctors gave out the medicines and surgical instruments brought from England.

Andrew had been taking a close look at a new house being built. They were using a combination of Tibetan and European building methods. Dengke is in an earthquake zone, and there was an earthquake in December 1992. So the houses must be built to cope with that. Thus the outside wall is not structural, just a shelter from the wind, rain and snow. Before the pump house could be erected, fibre glass cladding for insulation had to be cut in strips and threaded through the cavity walls. Mike Wisheart still wondered about the siting of his 'Sun User' water heater system. Inside the hospital compound would be safer, but quite a way from the water source.

September 15 Five of our men were invited to the temple, to speak to the monks and lama about the Christian faith. They had heard of it, but had never spoken to Christians before. They know no relationship with the Father God. The monks have 25,300 rules to keep, and spend much time in recitation. They accepted some Christian literature and asked the visitors to go back on Sunday.

Peter Gunner, with some local energy, dug through the foundations, to bring the pipe into the hospital. The trench was finished, and water can be sucked from the weir into the building. The electrical work is all but finished, and Grant triumphantly turned on the main switch. It worked for ten seconds, then we had a power cut. There were yells of laughter! At the doctors' joint clinic, glasses were sorted into short/long sight and stored for distribution. Janet saw the leper lady's home —(lovely, too small to stand up in) and gave her a pair of specs and Vaseline.

The weather had taken on a new pattern of constant surprises.

Cloud gave way to sun, then a fierce wind and torrential rain, with two hours of power cuts, then it turned absolutely still and very cold. We donned extra jumpers and socks and kept our coats on to work in. No wonder the locals never discarded their clothes.

September 16 Radio China started its clamour, then broke. After 8 a.m. prayers and breakfast there was a united effort to try to finish painting at the hospital. The water pump was carrying water 280 metres. A wall had been built for the suction pipe. There was consternation at the end of the rainy day, when the engineers tested the water pump. No water came, only air. Had the system broken? They tried the pump again and again for twenty minutes. They decided to check the pipe, but the workers, assuming the weather had driven everyone back to the hostel, had rolled up the pipe and stowed it away for the night. Red-faced, the engineers shared the joke with the rest over supper. The foundations for the pump house were dug, and gradually filled with rainwater. The water tank was attached to the wall in the hospital room. But at the medical team clinic morning, the local school said they did not have time to allow the doctors in to do an asthma study, as they were busy with school exams. Perhaps future co-operation needed to be discussed at a higher level for better organisation of timing. The local carpenter had provided a beautifully grained rectangle of wood, onto which the lights for the operating theatre were attached and switched on. It was time to start transferring equipment from the hospital to the kindergarten. We started with the bamboo ladder. The two delightful Tibetan teachers were so eager to help improve their workplace. The room was a cobwebby, sooty, dingy place. Through an arch, wood was stored for the fire. There was no light and no water. We would need to carry buckets from the hostel wash-house. The children had left, so we started washing down. It felt more like chimney sweeping. The blackened walls, gritty with soot, needed two washings and some rendering. The real transformation was to start the next day.

September 17 The teachers had told the children to go home as they arrived at school, and they devoted their day to placing tables and ladders for us to balance on, holding paint pots; and they provided Mandarin drink and apples for our refreshment. The local Head of Education and two other men watched, smoking their cigarettes. Two coats of white emulsion on the walls made an impressive difference. Yellow and red are favourite colours on buildings, so we painted the cleaned window frames a brilliant red and the bottom half of the wall a sunny yellow.

Up at the hospital, five solar panels were mounted. They could work the pump better than the generator, even though it was collapsing, so that had to be fixed. Two more rooms were kitted out with electricity and paint, one a minor operating room where stitches were weaved in and snipped out. Everyone worked so hard that the evening power cut meant a well-earned early rest.

September 18 It dawned a gentler day, clouds lifting. Andrew, still striding out having mapped the village, particularly wanted to see the house in Udren's village of Wan Tuo. Because of the bad weather over the last few days, we had not seen Udren, so Andrew, Rob, Sandra and Barbara went by jeep to visit. What a citadel that village is: nothing approached without everyone being alerted. Before we were out of the jeep, the children came leaping down the path, among them the Udren Rob had known two and a half years before, wearing her usual play clothes. Every alleyway and courtyard was awash with mud and effluent. The next project could include drainage experts, we thought. The children nimbly skipped from stone to stone, but often had to wade, ankle deep, through the quagmire. We had surprised them by this visit, and we saw Udren's family as they really lived. The white awning was gone, revealing their one-room home. Seats doubled as beds; a fine wooden box stood in the centre, acting as table and storage cabinet. We climbed up three steps into this room of three walls. At least it was out of the damp. A few planks and a large prayer flag separated them from the onslaughts of the elements. How they survived in winter one could not tell. A sheaf of barley was propped against one wall, some clothes piled in one corner, a basket in another; and a flat piece of wood on top of a large log provided a side table. The floor was of rammed earth. Here lived Udren with two big brothers, a big sister and her mother. We could not tell how they cooked —maybe they shared a neighbour's facilities, because bowls of warmed milk appeared from outside. The Polaroid photo taken a week back was mounted under some thick broken glass, next to a postcard Rob had given her, last time. We asked Udren to draw us a picture to take home. She hardly knew how to hold a pencil and just managed a slight squiggle. This bright-eyed child had no schooling, and any contact with stationery had been limited.

Barbara translated, as sweets and apples were offered round and more hot milk was poured from a blackened kettle. We had brought some jumpers as a present for Udren, but seeing their poverty, we left our coats as well. Our hearts ached as we left this desolate widow in such poverty. Surrounded by children, we walked to the edge of the village for a magnificent view of the Yangtze. Udren insisted on carrying my bag, and stayed as close as possible. Andrew and Barbara went back in the jeep. Rob and Sandra walked by the river, observing the farming methods; a dad with two daughters building a mud wall, and the logging industry. Dengke was well supplied with shops, which are mostly one small room with a wooden shutter onto the street. Customers stand on the roadside and lean through the window, pointing to the items they wish to purchase. There were some larger stores with glass cabinets, selling everything from combs to carpets.

The afternoon was spent finishing off all the activities started ten days ago. Everyone lent a hand as painters and 'cement-mixers'. The hospital and kindergarten finished inside and out, Tibetan artists painted a wonderful mural of flowers and leaves, clouds and sunshine, to surround a blackboard. The pump house was up, concreted round the base. The platform for collectors for the water heater was done. Nicky had enough sun today to measure the efficiency of her solar cooker. She concluded she needed a bigger umbrella. The water purifier worked, and a litre had boiled in three quarters of an hour. There had been a minor setback on the electrical scene as some plugs had mysteriously disappeared.

We finished the day with the usual storm for an hour; and then there was a party for the team, with games and party pieces that had us in fits of laughter. Everyone healthy again and relaxed, knowing that a good job had been well done. Mike, Gareth and Hazel had birthdays, and Sam and Madalyn their fourth wedding anniversary. We had much to celebrate. Everyone joined in wholeheartedly with old songs rewritten with a Dengke flavour: from the 'Dengke Loo Blues' to 'Mud, Mud, Glorious Mud'.

September 19 There was much clearing up to do before the grand opening at 3 p.m. We had made friends with an ex-teacher, who lived with her doctor husband and four year old son, in one room attached to the kindergarten. She had been consigned to a remote Tibetan area to teach. She had refused because it would have meant leaving her husband and son for months at a time, and because she was not fluent in Tibetan.

The last medical seminar went well. The local doctors were very keen on a return visit, and had made up a list of what they would like brought next time. One seventy-two year old man had travelled two days on horseback to see the European doctors, who were indeed able to help him. By 3 p.m. the hospital grounds were filled with colour, from the large red ribbon to the pink and greens of the girls and the finery of the boys, all holding flowers—real ones this time. Dahlias seem to grow well here. The speeches given expressed not just thanks but the trust that the Dengke folk and Chinese officials had toward us. There was an open invitation to return. Udren turned up wearing the pink cardigan given yesterday, and big brother had Rob's coat tied round his waist. We were given a bottle of milk and a plastic bangle. Why do poor people always give so much? The motto on our T-shirts read: 'One person cannot change the world, but we can change the world for one person.' The whole team longed to do that for the different individuals we had met —the trusting lepers aware of their hopelessness, and the unschooled 'Udrens' we saw around us. But they had also changed us in our appreciation both of our many blessings of health and comfort and shelter at home, and of their hardiness, generosity and friendliness. We were welcomed and honoured as if we were royalty.

Often our welcome and honour of strangers is so cold and apathetic. We thought we had come to give and, as is often the case, we received far more. The children wandered freely, often without supervision, round the town and in the countryside, responsible, needed members of their society. There seemed to be no fear of child molestation and kidnapping here. They loved to give. Two little girls came up to Hazel, gave her an apple, then ran off giggling. We were followed and watched by all ages wanting to help, though we had to keep an eye on the store room, as empty containers, be it of fuel or water, were in great demand. All our time in Dengke we were greeted by shouts of "Hello; goodbye; OK", whenever we emerged from the hostel. We had made good friends with Mr Umlaw, a Tibetan/English/Chinese speaker, who helped us in many ways, even with shopping, and would tell us if the price named by the shopkeeper was reasonable or too high. Our last phone calls by satellite ended, the equipment was packed away for the journey home. The spectacular scenery dimmed into a Tibetan dusk; then another dramatic thunderstorm. In the dining room we were invited to a local dance. The headmistress guided her lady partner round the room with military precision yet graceful gentleness. We had become so used to the men dancing together that even two males from our team dancing did not seem strange. We sat, arm in arm, with our waitresses, who had served us so hospitably. A party piece from the night before was performed, to the delight of both Chinese and Tibetan. It was a Dengke version of 'If I were not upon the stage, someone else I'd rather be'. Of course we had Gareth as the doctor, Grant as an electrician, Rob as an engineer, Janet as a carpenter and Madalyn as a painter. As the build up of their actions became ever more likely to collide with injecting, wiring, digging, nailing and slapping it on the wall, the audience clapped and howled with laughter. No one wanted to go home.

September 20 Sadly, it was time to pack our bags. After breakfast, the morning service was videoed, but it did not interfere with the worship. We shared the communion using steamed dumpling as the bread and boiled water for wine. We really knew we were one body in our communion together, remembering the Lord Jesus until he comes, and in all our teamwork, sickness, fun and dangers. What a privilege we had: to come and be in that place at that time. Would any of us be quite the same again? A brilliant, sunlit day called most of us out for a trek over the only bridge for hundreds of miles, straddling the Yangtze. Dengke would become a more significant town. It already boasted a hospital and school. Once the roads were built, to link up with the new bridge, its importance would soar. But for now we skipped the puddles down the high street and balanced our way along the earthen walls dividing the fields, past a white Tibetan tent, where a herd of yak grazed, and over the brown waters; and we panted our way up the Tibetan mountainside, to drink in the fantastic views across to Dengke nestling among its shady trees below the corresponding mountain opposite.

It was a photographer's paradise. Horsemen passed us, and two children holding hands smiled confidently at us. After lunch there was a last opportunity to take photos on our way to the hospital, where the bright sunshine made us screw up our eyes for the team photographs. Udren, her mother and goatherd friend were waiting with two bottles of milk. We took Udren to the shops and bought her some bright socks and material of her choice. Streams flowed through the town. It was the only running water, where folk washed their vegetables, and where now we saw children washing some clothes. Animals drank from these controlled streams, which were blocked further up the mountain at night. We passed the local butcher —the dead yak cut in large bloody hunks, its skin spread out for sale also. One man slowly swayed a tree branch over the carcass, its leaves rustling away the few flies keen to land. We bade farewell to our little girl and her humble mother as she set off for home. How unhurried their day is. Survival is their biggest pressure. Their village without electricity had no gadgets or conveniences. There was no diversion from the power of the elements around them, and hardly any shelter. They faced their frailty with hardiness; in the soft West we disguise ours with delusions.

Back at the hostel there were more team photos with the staff, and then began the loading of the lorries. The large, green Project Dengke boxes were lifted up and equipment not used, tool boxes, suitcases, and mats bought locally etc., were loaded inside them. The rest of the paint was left behind to emulsion and gloss the new school which was promised to be built. Solar panels, tanks, pipes, shed, and unlimited goodwill were left behind.

Many team members went visiting local folk to say goodbye. We had a celebration farewell meal with speeches, songs and games, and gifts were exchanged. One trader turned up with mats and rough turquoise pieces. Once they had coaxed the television into working order, we saw the Chinese television video of our stay, perched on the hard benches and floor. It made the bus seem so comfortable on the return journey, even though it was built for Chinese people with an average height of five feet (one and a half metres).

September 21 By 8.10 we had packed our last-minute things, breakfasted, and waved goodbye. There were sad farewells to the schoolgirls, who had become friends, the ex-teacher and the doctors. We remembered that the thunderstorm last night had ended with a wonderful double rainbow, and we took that as showing a promise for this place. We also had acquired a passenger —a Tibetan girl studying medicine at Dafu, who needed a lift. She sat, her head bowed, on the back seat, eventually accepting a bottle of water after much coaxing. However, our bus was still suffering from vertigo, even after two weeks of rest.

We had climbed less than an hour away from Dengke when the fuel pump broke. But what a wonderful view from our hilltop stop! A girl of about nine years was skilfully guiding her herd of goats, thrown into confusion by our sudden arrival. Responsibility gave these children great confidence; there was no generation gap. Everyone, young or old, was equally valuable and needed. Most of the children who swarmed up from a village below us were very poor. One was happily speaking into a tape recorder the alphabet and numbers to a hundred, so that Barbara could improve her Kumba dialect. Snow had fallen on the mountain tops around, reminding us of the need for speed to fetch in the harvests and to get over the mountain passes before they were blocked. An hour later, we were on our way again. The recent rains had two effects on the road. We rejoiced that the dust had been lain, but were aware of slithering round some bends. We passed herds of yak carrying the harvest of wood —such wonderful, willing beasts! We stopped by a fast flowing, crystal clear stream with an abundance of alpine flowers. Everyone waved as we passed. We supposed they take all this amazing scenery for granted; how well they blended with it. We wondered if any more work had been done to the bridge construction. It had not. Again, we stepped our way across the flow, to allow the bus to wallow through, as best it could. Somehow, it managed to pick up a rock between its double back right tyres. Another long stop as it was eventually dislodged. This seemed a particularly wild-looking area.

We were off again. The hostel had packed us a cardboard box of yak joints, dry biscuits and bottled water for lunch. The 2.20 p.m. breakdown required a new gasket. The fuel pump was cleaned out (our engineers offered to help). We had stopped in a village under some trees. Some of the team stretched their legs and discovered threshing being done by a hand-driven machine. Locals tried to sell us an old mat at an exorbitant price. It had been sat on by a lama, hence its incredible value. The bus was eventually mended by the use of a broken chop-stick used as a bung, and some oil bought from a villager. We just prayed it was suitable for a bus.

One mile further on, we were waved down. The bridge ahead had collapsed, and a large hole needed filling before the bus dare cross. With each of us carrying a couple of rocks from the nearby stream and laying them carefully on top of one another, the bus edged across slowly; we walked.

We passed a wide valley, totally uninhabited by people or animals, except for four yak carcasses picked clean by the vultures. It was a lone, dreary place. The next valley brought another breakdown, conveniently right beside some Tibetan tents with welcoming tenants. Animals grazed around. We were invited inside the woven, black yak hair tent; daylight showed between the woven sections. It was very smoky. Something was boiling in a huge pan on top of a mud stove. Leather bags, full of their belongings, and a wooden chest were at the back of the tent; the sleeping quarters surrounded the fire. Yak dung and brushwood were conveniently placed just outside the tent door. The guy ropes holding up the supporting poles were of black spun yak hair, which had a slightly greasy feel to it. Probably the whole structure was waterproof. Our Chinese drivers had tried all the tricks they knew to persuade the bus to restart: water and tea in the engine; then the fuel pump mended, even though it was with a chopstick. They had done a wonderful job, but now our engineers ventured to offer their services, hoping it would not mean loss of 'face'. They discovered a hole in a vital pipe, which, once carefully cut and refitted, made an enormous difference.

Six hours after leaving Dengke, we passed another vehicle. The air was so clear one could pick out individual bushes growing on the hills miles away. Our aim was to reach the Green Dragon Lake near Maniganggo, in daylight, to witness the stunning beauty of the glacier-fed lake. However, with the hold-ups and breakdowns, it was 6 p.m. before we slogged past a gang of twenty workers standing side by side, ramming down mud from a nearby hillside to form the wall of a new house. Horsemen passed us, and two children holding hands smiled confidently at us. The bus brought us, in the fading evening light, to a muddy meadow where a road was being built by workers who lived in a large tent. Concrete blocks littered the area, waiting to be arranged into a recognisable street pattern.

After navigating the path, we reached the 'bridge', a collection of planks, logs and sandbags over a rushing river —not for the faint-hearted! Over the hill, we were rewarded with a magnificent view. The gentle light softened the harsh lines of the rugged mountains and huge pines. The scenery could have been that of Norway, Canada or Switzerland. We breathed in the pure air as the colours faded, and we turned our backs on the lake —back to the bus, and returned in the

dark to the cold hostel. The one warm spot in the plunging night temperature was an amazing tin contraption in the kitchen, belching
smoke from its joints and steam from its kettles. But before we could
relax, we had to unload our bags for the night. Colin's bag was missing. A lorry driver had been hurt. Stitches were needed. At last, the
delayed lorries caught us up. Had Colin's bag fallen off on the bumpy
road? Had it been stolen? Had it been left behind with all the paint
and panels? Back in the cavern of the kitchen, from which emanated
light, heat and smoke, we sat on the benches. Too many colourful
dishes were brought for the table to hold comfortably, such was the generosity. We helped ourselves to rice, but it was not until we had actually eaten half the meal that we were handed the bowls.

September 22 Next day dawned very dry and clear. We climbed our
highest mountain peak: 4571 metres. No one felt breathless or had a
headache. The doctors explained that over the time spent at Dengke,
our bodies had adapted to the altitude and created more red blood cells
to compensate for the extra oxygen needed. Now we were fit and energetic. No wonder athletes train at altitude before the Olympics —a
natural way to improve physical performance. We drove through the
valley of the combine harvester. Suddenly there were screams from the
back of the bus. Three cockroaches had joined us on our journey. Two
were trodden on; one lived, to add to the excitement of another day.

After lunch we experienced such a range of weather: from hot sunshine to a fierce hailstorm, with hailstones so big that the bus had to
stop for fear of the windows being smashed. As the sun set, so the
thunderstorm sent the lightning from one mountain peak to another.
Then all was still, and because of the dustless, dry atmosphere, we saw
millions of stars. We were reminded of these verses in Psalm 8:

> When I consider your heavens,
>   the work of your fingers,
>   the moon and the stars,
>   which you have set in place,
> What is man that you are mindful of him…?

This project of purpose was also a project of perspective.

We crossed the bridge into Dafu and reached the hostel. A rushing river hurtled past the latrines; the planking vibrated with its impe-

tus. It looked as if some rice had been spilled at my feet in the lavatories but, as I looked, the white grains on the flooring were moving. They were the writhing bodies of infant maggots. I did not bother to shine my torch into the pit, I am sure it would have been heaving. The concrete space we will call the washroom had five taps leaning out of the pipes that snaked round the walls; some planking served as a stand for the enamel bowl provided in every bedroom. A single dim electric lightbulb added a meagre gleam. In the evening, the taps gave either cool or cold water. In the morning, one had the choice of hot or very hot.

September 23 We passed the Tibetan stone houses, now displaying signs of harvest, not just barley on the roof, but coming out of several of the windows. They seemed like little fortresses, with castellated tops, small windows and thick walls.

There was evidence of deforestation, tree stumps or scree on the mountainside announcing the reduction of vegetation which can hold the rocky soil in place. We sang *How great Thou art*, as we gazed in awe at the magnificent scenery. Half way through *And can it be...*, we came across long road works forcing the bus into the muddy depths of fields and river, and forcing us to skip our way, via stones and grassy clumps, until we could use the partly finished highway.

We climbed the mountain pass before descending to Kangding. We saw the Gonga Shan, covered in snow. At 7,500 metres it is the seventh highest mountain in the world, only one thousand metres lower than Everest. We stopped on a vast grassland where alpine flowers bloomed in abundance —deep blue gentians and edelweiss. Crickets, frogs and toads croaked their conversation in the absence of birdsong. Six tents were pitched in one valley floor covered with hundreds of yak. They even wandered nonchalantly over the road and played the game of 'waiting until the last moment to dodge the bus'. At six in the evening we arrived at Kangding.

September 24 We left Kangding at 7 a.m. for Luding, following the fast flowing river. Farming stretched almost to the top of the mountains. It must take so long to climb up to hoe or harvest. Our destination was Yaan, but if we could keep up the good timing, perhaps we might carry on and even reach Chengdu.... But that was not to be.

The towns grew larger, and each one had its own hydroelectric works. We could see the straight pipes streaking down the hillsides.

Knapsacked children, red scarves round their necks, walked in groups of twos or threes along the road to school. They were unaccompanied by adults, and as there were no pavements they were in constant danger from the heavy lorries hooting their way round corners. A flock of geese waddled, alert-eyed, across the road. Most people here were Chinese rather than Tibetan, and the women wore trousers and jackets, and had short hair.

Because of a desperate toilet stop, we reached the one way mountain pass system at 11.10 a.m., ten minutes after the barrier should have officially been shut, but with a few shouts of exhortation from our policeman, Mr Li, we were allowed through. We climbed above the cauldron of clouds, spuming and spewing white wisps of mist below us. Amazingly, miles from habitation, we passed a man walking a dog on a lead, a scene so out of place and so out of character, as dogs are usually eaten, not exercised. Always be prepared for the unexpected!

It had been raining heavily and, as we slithered to the top, we disappeared in a thick fog. It would be so easy to miss a bend and pitch over the precipice.

About one o'clock, we joined a queue of lorries, so got out to stretch our legs. The wet, putty-like, dampened dust provided an oozing, slippery surface, and we were soon to discover the real-life drama of heavy lorries on inadequate roads.

Our leader, Mel Richardson, takes up the story, which involved everyone on the team if not in rescuing, in nursing, encouraging or prayer.

Mountain Rescue

Mel Richardson

Life or death decisions that involve only oneself are perhaps difficult enough, but those that directly involve others are clearly likely to provoke an agony within one's spirit, usually only ever experienced by the like of generals, prime ministers and presidents. My agony was to be in the latter category. The incident itself I shall never forget.

I had just jumped out of the side of the team bus that was carry-ing us home through the mountains, and was staring in disbelief at the sheer drop where a lorry had just disappeared. Straight off the side! Nightmare stuff! With sickness in my stomach, I concluded that no one could possibly have survived such a horrendous accident.

"If anyone's alive, I'm going down," was the spontaneous and typi-cally sacrificial comment of chief medic Kevin Ilsley, who had now joined me at the cliff edge.

"If you get any closer to that sheer drop," I muttered to myself, "you'll be going down faster than you think." Slowly, the facts of the situation became clear. The doomed lorry and its three occupants had been trying to edge past another *dong feng* which had broken down and was blocking the greasy, wet, single-track highway. We had all been effectively in convoy, gingerly picking our way down this most danger-ous of passes, sometimes at over 4500m, on the easterly side of Kangding. It had been a 'white knuckle job', clinging on to our seats as we inched our way down, weaving past landslides with drops of thousands of feet a hair's breadth away —but who in their right mind would try to overtake? Perhaps familiarity breeds contempt. Incred-ibly, the driver who had started the trouble by choosing to change his wheel in the most inconvenient place imaginable, continued dragging on his cigarette, hammering the hub, apparently totally unconcerned for the apparent death of his colleagues. Being charitable, perhaps this was a form of 'mental shut-off' to traumatic circumstances —but I doubt it.

"Shout down for a sign of life," someone yelled, as about fifteen of the team now held on to one another, and their eyes followed the newly created corridor of ripped and torn bushes and trees that extended almost vertically below us. My agony was about to begin. Within seconds, an eerie scream echoed up through the mist, in reply to the demand for a response. Miraculously, at least somebody had survived. Momentarily, I turned to one side, wishing I could escape the decision I now had to make: to allow a rescue bid to go ahead (deploying brave but untrained, unequipped, inexperienced personnel) or to save the doctors from themselves (how ever well-intentioned). Surely it was madness to go down over the edge of that precipice? What would I tell their wives and families when their remains were transported home in a body bag.

"But why didn't you stop them? You were the end of the buck's travel. You were the one person who could have cried 'Halt'." Apart from anything else, the whole team had signed an indemnity form, in front of witnesses, agreeing that in just such a situation my word was final. Small consolation! A decision, and it had to be the right decision, was needed —and fast. As a Christian, I knew that special wisdom was required, irrespective of any ability one might have to make stable value judgements. Pacing up and down like a man in torment, my prayer was simple and direct: "Lord, let me think your thoughts, not my own."

As the parable of the Good Samaritan came to mind, my whole spirit became focused, and strangely warmed and willing, for what now lay ahead. OK, Kevin considered the men below to be his patients, but I considered Kevin and his doctors to be my 'patients' and my responsibility. I was not going to shirk that responsibility or throw my brain out with the bathwater, if you understand what I mean. I gave the 'green light' but urged extreme caution —I guess that was obvious, anyway. The team's two Chinese 'Mr Li's' (one a security policeman and the other a Foreign Affairs official) were both now much in evidence shouting in Chinese, presumably trying to clarify the confused situation. Since we had partly been doing medical work at Dengke, we had several doctors and nurses in our party and some medical supplies, such as the essential morphine and painkillers, which would now be 'rucksacked', in great haste. Swinging like demented monkeys from bush to precarious bush, the advance party of Kevin, Niels, Jon, and Arne, with no previous training of even elementary mountaineering techniques, made their way down the mountain face, rocks tumbling around them. Soon they were lost from view, with only swaying branches below us to signal locations. Then silence —and no further movement. When the bush swaying resumed some thirty minutes later, it was to herald the appearance of a blood-stained trucker being lifted (although still upright) up to the surface. The gasps of amazement soon gave way to professional action as nurses Barbara, Joan, Reiden, and 'physio' Val, coolly went about their business, aided and abetted by Peter, Geralyn, Rob, Sandra, John, and Colin. Meanwhile, Mike, Sam, Madalyn, Andrew, Lucy, Christine, Nicky, Paul, Hazel, Lily and myself hastily made preparations for the next casualty, who was to emerge dragged up, partly on his back, with severe internal injuries, a further thirty minutes later. He was in a bad way. Drips were set up, and the full resources of available medical manpower were deployed to save his life.

As agonising minute by minute passed, the word came up from the bottom of the cliff that the final trucker was still alive, but crushed into a tiny space in his cab, which by now was compressed into a matchbox, facing up the mountain, and in imminent danger of toppling down completely to the river at the bottom of the ravine. Jacks were sent down, and manpower reinforcements (which included Sam, Grant, Gareth, and Wei Shen, who got lost and returned) to force the cabin apart, so that the man's trapped leg could be released. Grant struggled with the jack, knowing that at any moment a huge log perched ominously above him could fall and obliterate both of them in a fraction of a second. Arne set about making a branch and coat stretcher, and the rest of the medical team worked frantically on the patient, who perhaps thought he must be dreaming as he was literally plucked from the jaws of death.

As he was dragged free, word was sent up to the surface that they would make their way to our right as we looked down in their direction (but hidden from our direct view). They were trying to find a less severe route back up. Peter and I decided to try and get down to meet them by scouting a pathway from a different angle. We tracked our way downwards, passing near a waterfall that was making everything even more slippery, desperately trying to find an easier way. We travelled for about a mile without getting the result we wanted. There was one gully with a stream tumbling down through it, but the final part (to those coming up) would have been another sheer rock face. Later on, having another attempt, I nearly tumbled down it head first, and decided to heed my own advice originally given to Kevin. 'Extreme caution' meant extreme caution. This mountain could still kill, and the light was beginning to go down.

Wearily moving back up to the rest of the team, I was informed that those still down had decided to come straight back up via the original route. As the first two injured were patched up the best we could, they were sent off to the nearest hospital. Preparations to receive the final casualty then started. A totally exhausted medical team, aided in the last few metres by fresh helpers, finally got the semi-conscious driver to the surface after four hours of dedicated team work. After much medical checking, and with drips held high above his head, we lifted and rolled this final survivor into a waiting Land Cruiser, ready for his mercy dash down off the cliff.

As a poignant footnote, it was interesting to learn from the stretcher bearers that, on the way up, Gareth slipped badly and started to fall, but the trucker writhing in agony grabbed his arm, as if to save him. Surely his unspoken message to us was, 'I thank God you are here helping me, but I too would have helped you if the roles had been reversed.' For us, the whole project, and not least the final incident, was a wonderful example of international friendship and co-operation at its best —expressed not just in words but in action. Above all, God protected each one.

Sandra Watson's Story resumes:
All thought of reaching Chengdu that night faded after four hours of rescue and another hour just getting down the mountain pass. We had to stop at the barrier, the opening of which had been delayed three hours because of the rescue. There was such a backlog of traffic to come through before dark that we piled into a roadside cafe and enjoyed the most delicious meal. It took one and a half hours for the Land Cruiser to get the injured man to Tien Tien hospital. Arne and Wei Shen accompanied him, holding an intravenous drip to combat the inevitable shock. It took twenty five minutes to find a stretcher and carry him up to the second floor of the hospital, put him to bed and make sure he was comfortable —all this after the patient had paid to be allowed in. His gratitude knew no bounds, as he was sure he would have died in the truck had the team not come to his rescue.

September 25 We left the enveloping smog of the factories in Yaan. The roads improved, population increased; and the countryside became flatter. We passed one lorry gasping its last, as it squatted on its haunches, its bonnet in the air: the proverbial straw had broken the camel's back, and its overloaded cargo was spilling over the road. One lorry was on its side, its load had shifted as it went round a bend. The neat fields, manicured and nurtured by diligent workers (aided by the occasional water buffalo) increased as we approached. Greyness heralded the environs of Chengdu. Arriving at 2.30 p.m., we all felt out of place among the golden pillars, marble floors and en suite rooms of the Jing Jiang Hotel, with a *shantung* clad lift operator; tablecloths; mail from home; and other Europeans looking rich, tall and foreign to us. I think we all echoed Hazel's preference to still be in Dengke rather than a Western hotel. But we were glad to have a shower again. The strain of the 200 metre precipitous rescue began to have its effect. Arne became ill for two days, partly through exhaustion, and as a stomach reaction to the responsibility and distress all the rescuers had experienced. Grant became very ill with pneumonia, only just able to walk slowly with Rob carrying his bag, four days later, when they flew out together to Hong Kong. It took him another six weeks to fully recover. Several team members were dogged by stomach upsets long after they reached home. Gradually the team parted, some through Hong Kong, others through Guanzhou; some stayed on to see the container on its way, others to stay in Chengdu to study or teach. An invitation to return was issued by our Chinese officials, who had become our friends. Such was the rapport between the team, and so strong the desire to continue the friendship exchange, that many of us look forward to another Project Dengke.

Chapter Seven

Andrea Bransford's Story (1999)

At the age of eighteen, my heart discovered the Tibetan people —so much that I wanted to go right then to Tibet and share with them the 'Good News'. Little did I know that eleven years later that opportunity would arise most unexpectedly.

Of course in everything we would be very careful to follow, and not break, the laws of China, our host country.

At the age of twenty, I went gallivanting alone across the Pacific, via an air courier, to Hong Kong. The same day as I arrived, a team arrived from England. Those who were coordinating our activities placed me in the same lodging as this team. In the bunk next to me, in a Chinese apartment in Kowloon, was June, a British lady who would visit me in Switzerland five years later, and invite me to join an excursion to China/Tibet ten years later. The message of faith was divinely being prepared in a special way, specific to the people of Dengke.

During the next few years of university, I studied the history of religion in China, Asian history, the Mandarin language, and any other courses I could find that filled my mind with knowledge of the people that I longed to visit. In 1994, I began two years of research for an international prayer project, during which I often found myself emotionally involved with the ethnic groups I studied. My heart yearned to tell them of the joy and love of God, and that research tied me to the people in a spiritual way somehow. The prayer profiles that I wrote on

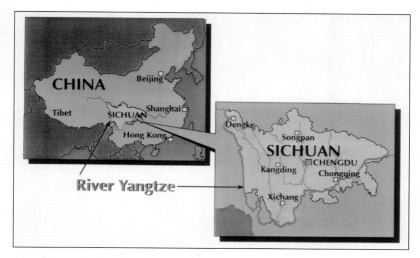

Above: Dengke location map

Below: Schematic showing locations and distances of Dengke from Chengdu

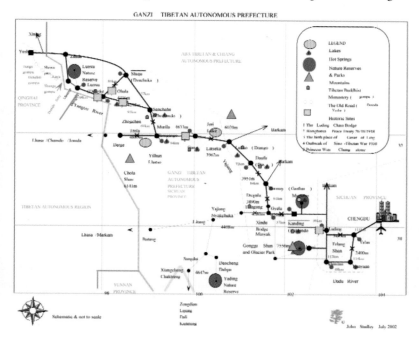

Above: Project Dengke Team 1995

Below: Project Dengke Team 1992

Above: Project Dengke Team 1999

Below: Erlang mountain rescue road

Scenic view of Sichuan mountains

Insert: Winding mountain roads

Above: Sandra shocked and praying during the 1992 mountain rescue

Below: View of Dengke from across the Yangtze River

Mel and Ang Luo with Dengke Valley behind them

Dengke children waiting for the drama presentation

Above: Horse riders in Bengda

Below: Mel with Dengke children

Opposite page: Dengke children welcome the team

Above: The famous Dengke loos (see Appendix B)

Below: Colourful Tibetan dancing girls

Colourful male dancer

Above: Close up of Tibetan girl and her colourful turquoise headress

Below: Yak

Colourful Tibetan
girl dancing indoors

John Studley mapping locations
with satellite tracking equipment

Above: Dengke flowers

Below: Dengke flowers and butterfly

Sichuan Berries —
painted by Kathy Wallace

Berries.

Lychees.

Centre: Dengke House — painted by
Vera Poole

Below: Dengke Flowers — painted by
Vera Poole

Above: Solar panel and windmill tests

Below: Designing and building in situ a pultruded reinforced plastic bridge

Above: Tibetan girls bucketing water in the traditional way
Opposite: Mel tests a 'Stirling Principle' water pump

Above: Colin and Sam test a solar water purifier

Below: Mike examines water pumps

Above: Heart patient on a bed

Below: Val and Janet with Shumsa, a leprosy victim

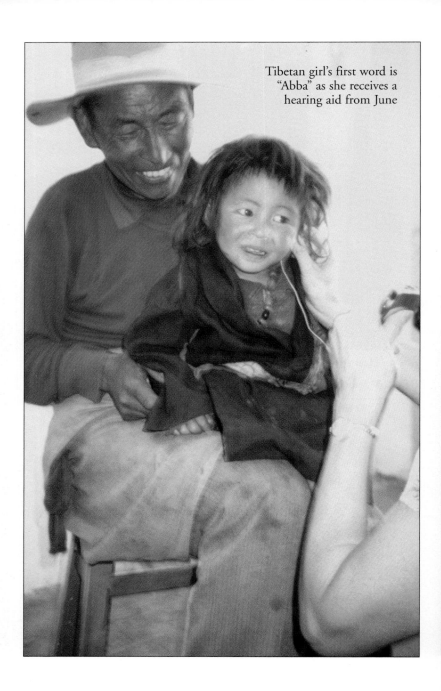

Tibetan girl's first word is "Abba" as she receives a hearing aid from June

Above: Val and Shumsa become close friends

Below: Leprosy patients need love, care and hope

Above left: Peter and Morna discuss plans with 'OJ', a dedicated local doctor
Above right: An artist paints the side of a house
Below: Val helps bathe wounds and sores

Sheer delight as June
prescribes a solar hearing aid

Above: Jack checks the work of local Dengke school children

Below: Jill trains a local doctor to perform basic dentistry

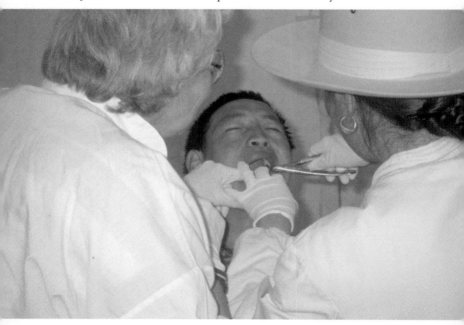

Above: As dusk falls, Andrea and team members present a dramatic presentation of the story of creation, in the School yard

Below: Keith, Rob & John line up with locals in Bengda. (Insert: Glyn)

Above: Stunning views of Bengda mountainside

Below: Keith ponders fishing 'Tibetan style' using dynamite stuffed in a beer bottle!

Above: Water powered flour mill

Below: Mel and Robert with Udren the little girl who inspired Project Dengke

Above: Steve conducts communion for team members in the local woods

Left: John anticipates 'Wok Delights'

Below: Black Panther rock band perform their tribute to Project Dengke

Above: Horn players

Below: Lily and Arne discover the music to the Kangding Love Song inscribed on a Luding monument

Above: The Dengke old cinema donated as the location for an International Friendship Centre and Orphanage

Below: The possible look of a future International Friendship Centre and Orphanage

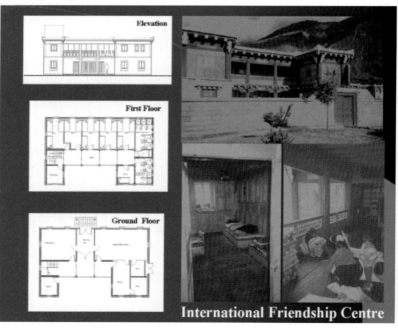

hundreds of ethnic groups were filled with God's heart of love for his children.

When I was presented by my friend, June, with an invitation to *Project Dengke 99*, I had no idea what I could contribute. I am not a scientist, environmentalist, surgeon or nurse, and they already had the teachers that they needed (not to mention that, after teaching all year, a teacher does not typically volunteer to teach in his/her spare time!) With what little I had to offer, I sent an email to the leader and submitted an application to him, along with my resumé. In all honesty, I did not have much faith and would not allow my hopes to be raised. Several days later, he wrote to me with the idea of communicating their health, medical and environmental messages via drama! He had noted on my resumé past experiences of leading drama teams to other countries —something that I thought would be too bold in China. The exciting part was that he also mentioned, whilst respecting and upholding the local law, communicating the message of our faith —a faith that welled up in my heart, and prepared to explode into the hearts of the Tibetans. Years before, the people had asked the team about their 'Western faith'. And so began a *true* story, of our journeys through the wilds of China and Tibet....

From the moment that I left my home in Denver, Colorado (leaving my fiancé to prepare our wedding and honeymoon!), it took nine days to arrive in the village of Dengke —which is minimal compared to the trip back to Denver, that took an entire twelve days. My first stop on the long journey was in England. Once I was there, as I looked around me at the faces of the people that I had been emailing for several months, I wondered what kind of natural talent was there that I could work with. I did not know many people, and I silently watched their mouths move just as mine did, but every word of theirs sounded a bit funny to me. Before I could blink (so it seemed), it was my turn at the team meeting. I had requested some time to talk to those who were interested in drama. I was quite humoured as I watched every engineer, doctor, nurse, pastor, scientist, professor, and retiree act as though they were blowing a bubble that popped in his/her face; pretending to walk a big dog that pulled at their arm; and then act as if they missed a gear while going uphill in a standard car. It struck all of us as funny when they did not know my word 'shift' for changing gears. After another childish activity and an explanation of the drama team goals, I passed around a sheet for those who were interested, and every person in that room signed up as a willing volunteer for the drama team —with the exception of one of the photographers, whom we needed to take pictures anyway. I was delighted by the simplicity of the team, and their willingness to look like complete idiots.

I had been preparing various dramas for several months, according to the needs of the Tibetan and Chinese people, and according to the suggestions of our leader and others who had been on this journey to Dengke before. My fiancé and I had done the recording for an environmental piece, which communicated the importance of preserving the forests, but I still had the 'faith message' to work on when I arrived in England. Neil Swettenham, a drama professor at a university in England, volunteered his services as a 'sounding board' and ended up helping with the recording. Neil and I worked from 4 p.m. straight through until midnight one night, putting together the pieces of music which applied the desired emotion to the message of the Creator God and his loving plan for his children. We pulled out old vinyl records, cassettes, CDs and a keyboard, and also depended greatly on prayer. Prayer was an important part of this preparation, because God was certainly with us, and the music was especially anointed and powerful —a feat that we surely could not pull off in our human strength.

On the flight to Beijing, I began to meet those who would play different characters, in order to walk them through the drama and introduce them to their role (via Walkman and a mini disc player). Although some did not quite have that ear for music, all team members were enthusiastic and willing. I was thankful to God for that. They had no idea what they were getting themselves into. I was hoarse by the time we arrived in Beijing, but pleased that the team was excited about the message.

I had seven days of travel in which to teach the team two extensive dramas, and it turned out that delays along the roadside seemed to be the best opportunities for practice. It is hard to believe that some parts of the 'road' were privileged enough to be called a road. It had rained recently, making the already dangerous roads even more dangerous. The road between Chengdu and Dengke made us sing —for a lack of anything else to do, to keep our minds off 'the long and winding road... that leads... to Dengke'; we sang choruses, then proceeded to re-write the words to every Beatles song that we could think of, as well as numerous others from the 70s. *Slip slidin' away* was a popular one that we always found ourselves singing, as we were flung from one side of the bus to the other, holding hands with those sitting by our side and whispering a prayer. Some people gasped quietly, some yelped or screamed, others cried. And we all survived, some more painlessly than others, but all were survivors nonetheless. I have travelled what are considered to be the most dangerous roads in the world —roads with sheer drops and numerous records of trucks and buses going over the precipices, and roads which have been written up as the most dangerous roads, in travel books. However, none of them even remotely compared to the muddy, winding road through the mountain passes to Dengke. Rumour has it that a tunnel through these mountains is soon to be finished, so that others venturing out to Dengke will not have to experience such a test of faith. I honestly believe that angels' wings were holding our tyres onto the road so that we would not fall off the mountains.

We usually set off around 9 a.m. on our daily bus journeys. Of course we were scheduled to leave at six, but were delayed due to the replacement of bus tyres, arguments about whether the drivers wanted to even drive us to Dengke, etc., and we usually decided for a stop to sleep around 11 p.m. Here are some thoughts from my journal, written on the bus:

16 July Chengdu, Sichuan Province, China. Watching the sea of bicycles, insane taxi drivers creating new lanes and nearly bumping the bulleting bikers. Walking across the multi lane roads, holding my breath; randomly pointing at the Chinese characters on the menu, and wondering what kind of food I had just ordered; sadly passing by the live ducks with their feet tied for roasting; shutting out the deafening tone of vendors in the store-fronts; feeling completely helpless when the Chinese ask questions and anxiously await a non-existent reply....

July 17 Now on our way to the Tibetan plateau. We have just reached the hills, and the sights are truly amazing. I did not bring enough film! The bus bottoms out on every bump, and they just filled two drums of diesel that are riding on top of the bus. Rather disturbing. Foreigners seem to be a novelty. Little straw hats are sporadically dotted in the corn and rice fields. Oxen and ducks bathe together in small man-made ponds. It looks to me as if it is the women in the sun-beaten fields, and the men sitting around shirtless, chatting in small groups in shaded areas. Both men and women do road construction. Although many men are chilling out in the shade with their buddies, I have seen one or two helping in the fields, carrying water in two buckets balanced at the ends of a pole, carried across their shoulders. The women do this, too. Little boys are with their fathers, and little girls with their mothers, learning the tricks of the trade. Although most houses are made of stucco or adobe or brick, occasional ones are of wooden planks. They do not seem to be kept up as well. It is interesting that some of the roofs are flat, with ridges round the edges. The rainwater is held there on the roof, perhaps cooling off the inside. Fields are beautifully groomed and artistically designed; few are rigid and straight. Rice fields are outlined by an occasional row of corn stalks. From above, it would look like a mosaic, or if coloured, like a piece of stained glass. Beneath the shadow of the rows of corn stalks, other crops are harvested. The people have made good use of every inch of soil. The vegetation changes quite often as we rise, little by little. We are driving through ferns now.

It is lunch time so more people are taking a break —having a smoke, playing cards, splashing themselves with water, hanging out with the family, drinking a warm drink, playing mahjongg and another board game that looks like chess. And yet some carry on with their work: hoeing, spreading corn kernels out to dry, hauling heavy baskets of crops on their backs, cooking, hanging out laundry, sewing, and feeding chickens. The children are riding their bicycles home from school now. They have little cartoon book bags. Some stop to put their feet in the stream. Ducks are absolutely everywhere —in the ponds, rivers, stores, gardens, markets, patios and, yes, even atop the buses! I am surprised that we have not had to show our passports anywhere. We are on a mud and rock road now.

Recovery from the toilet experience. VERY BAD. Stopped for a couple of hours after lunch to get a new tyre. Long wait on the road-side. Lunch was the absolute greatest —nice and spicy!

We are surrounded by green, lush mountains on all sides now, and our journey is being accompanied by a dirty river —quite wide and turbulent. Children are fishing amongst the rocks along the edges of the rushing water. As we disappear into the rising mountains, the vegetation gets greener, the air fresher, the river calmer and narrower, and the driving scarier. At this moment, I feel like I am in Bolivia again. It is breathtakingly beautiful. I cannot stop smiling.

19 July White-water rapids rush madly through the mountains, like painted clouds on the ground. Vibrantly coloured flowers naturally decorate the land. The road is made of packed dirt and is no longer muddy. That is comforting, considering our 'near death' ride to Kangding. It was a twenty two hour day, and a test of faith.

We are now approaching the Gye La Pass, just outside Kangding. We will stay the night in Lu Hue. It is now quite chilly. There are stone markers on the side of the road, that tell you how far you are from Beijing. Altitude now about 3000m.

At Gye La, the panoramic view is absolutely amazing. We are higher than the surrounding mountains, so everything is green and hilly. We have seen some scrawny yaks, and then one group of robust ones that were grazing around a nomadic tent. The life of the shepherd girls looks rather lonely. They are walking the sheep and the yaks. The men from this particular region wear a red yarn hair piece. They are zooming by on motorcycles.

20 July At Lu Huo (Drango). We are climbing up to 4633m today. I can only hope that my head holds together! Yesterday I did not do so well. Today we are going to Ganzi (if we ever leave), eating in Manigango, passing through Sanchahe (Chusumdo) and finally arriving in Shiqu, where they will throw a banquet for us.

On one of these long days of travelling, we were stopped in a long line of vehicles because a truck had slid and overturned. That one fell into the mountainside rather than off the mountain. During the delay, I visited a Tibetan family next to the river until we both ran out of mutual gestures and limited Mandarin. They enjoyed looking through my binoculars, and we took lots of pictures until I ran out of film. Then I headed back to the bus.... A natural drama teacher would look at this situation like so: truck overturned; an approximate six hours to right it; a terribly long time to just sit around and do nothing... DRAMA PRACTICE! And so we began our very first practice, and drew our first crowd. A drunken man even decided to join our team (would not get 'off stage'), so I positioned him as a 'tree', placing his arms in the air like limbs —and he did not move! He reeked of alcohol but seemed to enjoy being a good 'tree'. Our practice lasted until we all felt sunburnt, and then some settled into the buses for a long afternoon nap, while others wandered off for a hike around the area and searched for a makeshift loo. We could not do too much physical activity due to the effect of the high altitude.

22 July Ganzi. Yesterday we managed fifty kilometres in seventeen hours. The journey is obviously long, slow and extremely dangerous. The rain and muddy roads yesterday caused numerous accidents, one of which blocked the path for eight hours before they were able to right the overturned truck. Once we passed by, we sat for numerous long periods of time behind vehicles in front of us, which were stuck in muddy trenches. Thankfully none of our three vehicles got stuck, but we fishtailed slowly on the last hour of our journey to Ganzi, holding on for dear life and singing choruses (until the Chinese put on a loud movie in the bus). There were lots of laughs, and some tears, to relieve the fear of near death.

One of the drama teams performed a drama of dance and movement on the fifth day of travel. This was much to their surprise, and mine, too. We spent our 'free' day practising dutifully, since we were to perform that night at a banquet and I had not even finished choreographing it! The people of the village seemed to respond quite positively, applauding and sighing in the appropriate places, and were silent when needed. There were many cultural aspects to consider, and I was pleased with the response of our first crowd. They openly showed emotion throughout the whole thing, and rejoiced with us. The people were both Tibetan and Chinese.

That same evening, the Tibetans performed for us in their brightly coloured traditional outfits. Long, fluorescent pink sleeves slapped at the floor as the Tibetans spun, kicked, leapt and tapped to the live Tibetan band. After a while they wanted us to participate, so their dancers invited us to dance with them, both slow and fast dances. To touch the people was to realize that they were corporeal. To ask their name was to realize that their language was real and completely different. To discover their names (after much laughter and misunderstanding) was to discover Tibet, which to me had always been a distant dream. And, of course, to eat their food was to meet a taste bud challenge, especially the yak-butter peanuts that they had served that evening!

Our final day of the journey brought us into the village of Dengke.

We rode parallel to the Yangtze, with people trailing the buses, smiling and waving, and following us to the compound where we would spend the next two weeks. The people who awaited us were of the most beautiful that I had ever seen outside books. Their vibrantly coloured clothes and headgear could have lit up a moonless sky at midnight, and their smiles reflected the brilliance of God's heart when his children please him. Although I was excited beyond belief, I was also exhausted and ready to wind down after nine days of travel.

We climbed up to our assigned rooms at the compound, and selected which hay mattress we would sleep on. After dumping our gear, we took a tour of our living conditions. Fifty yards from the building, there were pig stalls, and a loo for each gender (we did have to share a common pit that lay below the squatty potties, though —quite a stench). Fifty more yards up the hill, thankfully, a family had volunteered their water to us. They brought it daily from the only faucet in the village, which a former British team had installed several years before. In their home, a large kettle with a fire brewing underneath kept a portion of the water quite hot for our bucket baths. We wore flip flops inside the water room, since there were only dirt floors; and the guys used the main room for 'bathing' while the girls tramped another 20 yards across a stream to a separate, somewhat private room (somewhat, because of the windows that passers-by sometimes stopped to peer into).

Of course we all needed to go to the loo the instant we arrived, but due to the hordes of people whose eyes followed us every step we took, we waited… and waited, and waited, and waited. Finally the crowd dwindled, and I escaped to the loo. I calculated the distance of each foot on either side of the reeking hole (so as to not fall in the pit) and prepared to… and then I heard noises, yes, even giggles. I looked up to find several wee girls watching me straddle! There is nothing quite as intimidating as somebody watching you when you are trying to go, so all motion was halted, and I exited, awaiting a more private moment —few and far between.

The next couple of weeks were full for me. We held group drama practice at sunset by the Yangtze, and individual practice with my new actors and actresses during the day. We had team meetings at night, and listened to all that God had done through the teams that day.

A friend and I were invited to a Tibetan home one evening in our second week in Dengke. They brought out plates of yak meat, pork fat and something unrecognizable, and then came the 'chung' —alcohol from barley. I did not think it was very strong, and figured about five glasses of that was equivalent to one glass of wine, but some present were affected quite quickly. And then the people sang for the next three hours. I loved it. Their voices were incredible and the words so meaningful. The first song and toast was sung, "You are welcome to my country. Make this your home." It was the beginning of a wonderful cultural experience. The words were deep and moving, about friendship, about family, and about life. "Friendship is like flowers. If only one blooms, that does not mean that springtime is here; but when many flowers bloom together, then we know that spring has come." It was not springtime in Dengke, but I felt spring in my heart.

27 July I crossed the bridge and met Tibetan horsemen along the way, who stopped to talk, and had heard that the doctors were here. June said that one man had travelled for five days after he heard it shouted over a mountain that we were here. How humbling. We came to work alongside the Tibetan doctors, to work *with* them, rather than in their place. The Tibetan people taught us about medicinal herbs, and we were able to teach them to use a stethoscope. Numerous people, especially children, were brought into the hospital for cleft lip surgery. Their countenance changed within a few days, and they had confidence in public that they had not known before. Abscesses the size of soft balls were surgically removed. And many had their hearing tested and were given a solar hearing aid. Indeed, the deaf heard! One older man, who had traveled for days from within Tibet, saw me filming with the television crew out in a field along the Yangtze. He came running across the field, with his pony trotting after him, yelling something that none of us could understand. When he got closer, we saw what he was trying to tell us. He had the solar panel hanging around his neck, and he could hear. Even now, the tears and a smile from ear to ear come to my face, as I remember this old man glowing from the miracle of sound, smiling broadly with his few teeth, and muttering sounds that he himself could hear. We could not understand his words, but we knew his heart. May he know the God of salvation, who answers prayers.

29 July One afternoon, several of us dared to venture further down the road across the bridge to Tibet. We went to the beach along the

Yangtze, that was candy coated in metamorphic rocks. As I looked around at the surrounding hills and dipped my toe into the Yangtze, the Vineyard song *Shout to the Lord* rested sweetly in my heart. On the Dengke side, as we practised 'Creation' last night at the bridge, the sun was setting into the mountains to the west, and the moon was rising like a saucer over the mountains in the east. It was phenomenal. I asked the team to look at the beauty of God's creation as we closed in prayer. We were all awed by the works of his hand.

As the drama team leader, when my actors and actresses were busy with other work, I, too, was free to participate in other projects. One of those days, I decided to work with the engineering team; however, I knew very little about installing electrical wires or about the installation of a windmill panel, so I decided to be a Tibetan lady. We all had a good laugh as I tried to help the ladies load tiles onto the eco-house roof. One of them held up the basket to put on my back, and they just fell about laughing. They tied the thick rope around my neck and shoulders, and I followed the line of beautiful Tibetan women to get cement roof tiles piled into my basket. I did not notice how many the little man had loaded into the basket until we made it to the roof, where another lady was unloading them (and giggling at me). There were only TWO! And then I counted those in the basket of the girl behind me: SEVEN!! When I pointed out that she had seven and I had only two, I demonstrated that I am a complete wimp, and we all had a good laugh. The sun felt like oven coils, but the temperature was perfect — in the 70s (F).

While working on the roof, a girl had to hold my hand going up and down the ladder. 'Ladder' here means the half-logs tied together with twigs and set on a 45 degree slope up to the roof. To me, it felt like a swinging bridge, and I was completely dependent on others to hold my hand and go up and down with me. I had to practise a few times before I tried it with concrete roof tiles! I could not do it without the people, and this dependence on them broke down the cultural and lingual barriers. I felt like a part of them. Even at work, the ladies wore their gorgeous hats, which were connected to their necklaces made of turquoise, amber, silver, and bone, most of which are unusually expensive. It is said that they wear their wealth on their heads and in their hair.

On other days, I helped the construction crew tie thick steel wires together for the solar panel; and, a couple of times, I was able to join the recreation team for a bike ride. That was exhilarating. One evening, at dusk, we went for a ride. We watched the sunset and rode on a foot path through a cornfield, then down to the riverside, a bit further from where my feet had trodden the time before. It was magnificent. On one of our free weekends (a rarity), I had the absolute best day of the whole trip. I shall record it straight from my journal so as to capture the moment:

31 July Today was the absolute best day that I have had so far. Ang Luo took four of us up the mountain that serves as a backdrop to Dengke. It was simply amazing. We went native style —straight up the mountain! I am sure there were easier paths around the mountain, but yes, we went vertical. The views were, of course, mind-bogglingly beautiful, with the Himalayan griffins flying overhead, and some even flying below us, and with the gorgeous Tibetan mountains rising majestically behind the immediate hills. We first saw the caves that monks live in for three years, three months and three days in seclusion as they study to be lamas. We headed up to the caves, were able to go inside one, then were going to go up to the top where there were prayer flags, but a monk stopped us. He said that we could not go higher; only their religious people could go to the top. They did, however, permit us to go up the rocky side of a cliff at a thirty degree angle (it had a wire to help us along); and there we saw two most fascinating monk caves. The small rooms where the lamas-to-be stayed, for years at a time, were very simple, with a sheepskin for sleeping on.

From there we slid down the mountainside to meet the nuns, who all looked like the monks since their heads were shaved. We sat looking out over the Dengke valley and Tibetan foothills, and ate the treats that the nuns brought. They were quite fascinated with us. We ate something called *tsampa*, which was barley flour, yak butter, sugar and hot water mixed together and eaten by the clump. I was glad that they gave us apples and little sweets, too! We had brought some candy and biscuits for them from the village. We then headed down the same way we had gone up —vertically! We said hello to the sheep, yaks, and herders along the way and said goodbye to the most gorgeous views of Tibet that we saw during the whole journey. My body and lungs were happy to have Sunday to rest!

I wrote a song that evening, as I reflected on my day's experiences:

There is a longing in my heart
And I'm thinking of you, my Lord.
I watch the birds soar in the wind
Tibetan eagles and the doves... flying high.

I see your smile in every cloud;
I'm hearing you whisper in my ear.
We walk along the river side,
And I feel that you are near... by my side.

And the birds sing out your name
And the flowers sing of the same
And all of my heart, all of my mind,
All of my soul longs for you...

Dengke at night was stunning. Two of the scientists found me staggering in awe with my mouth agape, and began to point out things that my pea-brain could not contain. What I saw at night was clearer than any planetarium that I have ever set foot in. Pictures in the sky. I could only think, "My God, how great you are", over and over, every night. If I were not already a believer, I would have looked up on the first clear night and fallen on my knees to receive the Maker of heaven and earth into my tiny life. To think that he is concerned with me is humbling.

After the first week and a half, my drama team became tired. Their activities of the day done, they went straight into dinner, after which there was no break before we would start practice. After major face surgeries, hours of manual labour, full days of teaching, and hours of seeing people in general, the team was exhausted. And then we lost a character. One of the team was tragically affected by the altitude and had to be evacuated.

A couple of days before the final rehearsal, I was asked to do a demo about germs, for the school children. Hmmm... invisible bacteria that make you sick. And so several of us prepared to be 'germs', and demonstrate the various ways that they make their way into our

107

bodies. Basic hygiene was an important thing to teach. We performed at the school that afternoon, and I can only hope that the kids got the picture and did not just get a good laugh at adults looking silly!

The big night finally arrived. Perhaps two hundred villagers showed up on the school grounds, where we set up our 'dress rehearsal'. It was possibly more like a true performance than the performance itself. This one was for the Tibetans, for the poor and rich, for the average farmer or merchant, for the people who wanted to know about our 'Western faith'. They were responsive. The *'Tree' Dance* drew a crowd, and the account of creation reached them, deep within. I introduced it: "This is a story of a Father's unconditional and perfect love for his children. It is a story of good versus evil; and a story of love, betrayal and forgiveness."

They smiled as the Creator created man and woman; they laughed as the Creator loved them, and showed them the lovely things that he had made for them; they were disappointed when man touched the forbidden tree; and they were unhappy when the 'toys' were affected by 'sin'. They were aching when these things formed a barrier between the Creator and his children; and then they watched the agony of the Creator's death because he took the blame for the children's evil actions. I could see it in their eyes, and the pictures show it in their faces. The message reached their hearts, their souls, and perhaps their hungry spirits deep within. Much to my amazement, there was no laughter when the Creator's power triumphed over evil; and, to my pleasure and surprise, they applauded stealthily when evil was bound and kicked offstage by the victorious Creator! The cast did excellently. I had no complaints, and was so pleased that my heart could burst. I felt humbled and honored that God would use us in such a task. The seed was planted. The people of Dengke know the story.

The next evening was our last night in Dengke, and it was the night of the big performance. I was nervous and excited, and dressed in a pink Tibetan shirt with sleeves to the floor. I rolled up the sleeves (so American of me), checked our props, asked how each cast member felt, and made sure everyone was OK, painted up the faces of our two evil characters, and then left it to Ang Luo to introduce the 'Tree' Dance. The Chinese government banned logging a few years ago, because of its effect on the environment. We tried to use movement and dance to reflect the effect of logging on the environment, and used replanting as one of the solutions. This appealed greatly to the Chinese, and moved the Tibetans emotionally. Then *Creation* was performed for the government officials that evening. Sometimes a message must start at the top and wind its way down into the population.

If it were not for the immense cultural differences that evening, it would have been difficult to leave Dengke. The people do not have the same sense of privacy that we do, so they would open the doors to our rooms just to have a look, to stare at us, to watch how we make a bed, pack and change clothes. There was no knock, no semblance of a warning, and lo! Your door was flung open, with people standing at the entrance staring at whatever you happened to be doing at that moment. Eyes! That is my last taste of Dengke —many watching eyes. This happened into the wee hours of the morning, since there were no locks on our doors. We would wake up to a squeak, hall light, and eyes.

6 August On the road again. Wow. I have VERY mixed feelings as we drive away from Dengke, heading back through the mountains on tiny dirt roads. I left some nice things with our xiao je (bell hop) this morning, along with a postcard from Colorado that I wrote to her —a small poem, to say 'thank you'. I realize that I did not establish relationships with the locals, except with the translator and the shopkeeper. Other than that, I just watched and observed, and interacted with whoever was around. Tears come to my eyes and sorrow to my heart. I will not see these people and this land again. Should it be so difficult to say goodbye to the ceaseless feeling of grit and dirt? To the hikes to that one faucet of running water to wash clothes? To the cat baths in a single bucket? To the sound of hawking and spitting from dawn to dusk? To constantly being accosted by kids saying, "hello, hello"? To the effort of boiling water just to have a drink? To being watched at all times, and surrounded when at a shop? But it is not the physical life that I thrive on. No, it is the closeness of a team and the joy we bring the people and the joy that they bring us. It is *friendship* that I will miss. The times of turmoil and difficulty and vulnerability have bonded us together, and none of us will ever be the same again because of it.

On the way out of Dengke, for the first couple of hours, people waved at us. Word must have got out that we would be leaving. Tibetans stood on their roof tops, out in their gardens, along the roadside, at their houses, and waved. We waved, too, with big smiles. Smiles of gratitude to these people for helping us change our perspective of the world; smiles of thankfulness that we were going home, and smiles covering the sadness, as we waved goodbye to people that we would, perhaps, never see again.

To take our minds off all that, and off the hazardous ride back to Chengdu, several of us acted out the actual script of *Romeo and Juliet* on the road side of each stop. The people thought we were ludicrous: reading a book and talking funny, then acting out the scenes. I just think we were losing our sanity! There were plenty of unwelcome stops, due to road construction …and our drum of diesel fell off the roof. For some reason, there was a dog tied to our roof, too. The driver must have picked it up in Dengke.

Since I felt like I missed out on getting to know Tibetans, I was delighted at the invitation to spend the night with one of our translators on our stop in Tawu:

7 or 8 August Tawu. 1:30 a.m. These people really do stay up all night! I am spending the night with Li and her family in a typical Tibetan home. It is beautiful. The Tibetans here in Tawu speak Mandarin. We arrived here at Li's house around 9.00 p.m., ate dumplings, drank some wine; then at midnight we were expected at a wedding festival! The house of the couple had several rooms set up with tables that ran parallel to the walls of each room. The tables were full of snacks, and each table had a bench on the side of the wall. They served *chung*, Tibetan tea (complete with yak butter) and *Sprite*. Of course, as usual (so I was learning), we had to sing. They, too, sang for us. It was hard to find a song we had in common, since the four of us were from Scotland, America, Singapore and Tibet. We finally sang *This is the Day* and *Amazing Grace*. I really enjoyed 'hanging out' in a small group and meeting new Tibetan people.

The journey continued from Tawu the next day; we stayed in Kangding the following evening, then had a long stop at the top of the Erlang Mountain pass. Because the pauses were so frequent, we were finishing the final scene of Romeo and Juliet there. I am sure the small crowd that watched was puzzled by the sword duel and the stabbings of the grand finale! We all needed a little entertainment by that time.

The remainder of that long trip home is a blur. I got altitude sickness; fainted in a restaurant on the side of the road; was carried to the other bus, and lay there until we reached our stop that evening. Rumour has it that there was no life in me, no colour at all, and that I scared many people. Then I was lugged to a bed and set down for the evening in an unknown town, some 40 km before Ya'an. I dreaded the ride into Chengdu the next day, and did not eat for the second day in a row. The team went to a banquet that night, while I stayed in bed and called home. I managed to keep down fried chicken the next day. We rode around town in rickshaws pulled by older, bony, Chinese men; sipped coffee in a coffee house, and went to a pizza cafe for dinner.

Upon arrival in Beijing, one other team member and I dumped our luggage in airport storage and took a taxi to the Great Wall. When we got there, we had one hour to climb the steep, uneven steps and take in the breathtaking sight. It was overwhelming. That very wall that we were standing on extended 2500 km. It was strong and majestic. Beyond the peak of the third mountain was rubble, which seemed most exhilarating to climb, so off we went through the rubble to the next summit. I am not sure how many miles you could see that day, but I felt like we could see Chengdu from up there. The climb back was so steep that many people grabbed the handrail and climbed down backwards, but we had a bus to catch for the ride back to the city and were running down! Beijing is well documented in other books, so I will not waste space and bore anyone with the details here, apart from to say that it takes more than six hours to see it! We got to the hotel at midnight and flew to London the next morning. Ironically enough, *Shakespeare in Love* was the film played on the plane on the route back, and our own quasi-Shakespeare Company reminisced about our tiny production during road stops. It already seemed so far away....

March 31, 2000 Reflections. I look back on that journey, back in time, and I see faith. I see people who, during my earlier research, had been shadows in a book. Perhaps, before, I had thought of them as foreigners, aliens, and strangers, or just another ethnic group. Now they are real people, equals, peers, and friends. I could not fathom a nomadic lifestyle until I befriended the nomads. I could not understand the Tibetan people until I befriended a Tibetan. I see now that we are different, but we are equal. We are all the Creator's children, truly loved by the Creator. And it is a true story that everyone should come to know... someday.

Another Vineyard song that wells up in my heart as I reflect on Tibet is, *I could sing of your love forever*. If you know it, please sing it for me, and most of all, for our Creator God.

Chapter Eight

John Milton Whatmore's Story

We have been travelling for six and a half hours along mountainous roads —that is Rachel Pinniger, Dee Larkham, Duncan Hanton, Sarah Mather, Colin Hart and myself. We have just finished the child vaccination project in Derge and, after nearly three months in China, I am at last going to see our base camp at Dengke. Now we had come to a deep valley, at the bottom of which, though still unseen, was the Yangtze. The track hugged the side of the valley walls, winding at precarious angles and slowly descending to the valley floor. Then, as we rounded the umpteenth z bend, I saw the mighty river the Chinese call Chang Jiang (Golden Sand). It was 4.30 p.m. and the sun was glinting on the waters as they snaked into the folds of the mountains. Almost immediately, I had my first view of Dengke, a collection of houses and trees on the western bank of the great river Yangtze. So this was where we were to put our hovercraft on the water, and start our great adventure.

That was an entry from my diary of the British Hovercraft Expedition to the source of the River Yangtze in 1990. The main party had been in Dengke for several days by the time I joined them with the medical team. In those days most of the villagers had never seen Europeans before, and were shy, but friendly towards us. We were camped on the banks about a mile from the village, and whilst pleasantries were exchanged, we were not allowed into the local hospital, school or monastery. We were meant to be in Dengke for about four days, while we put the hovercraft through the first water trials but, due to an accident on the river with the larger of the two craft, most of us were there for two weeks.

Little did I know at that time that this small, remote village was to be so much a part of my life for the next nine years. It was clear to one or two of us that, although a pocket of the community in the east of the village seemed comfortably off, most of the population of Dengke endured a low standard of living. It was thought that the village would benefit from some high technology, and friendship. So it was that I had the privilege of helping Dr Mel Richardson and Rob Watson to set up and establish *Care & Share Foundation*, a British charity. The Foundation has enabled several projects to be carried out over the last nine years. It has been my pleasure to return to China many times and to visit Dengke in 1992 and 1995.

The village is situated on the banks of the Yangtze where it forms the border between Sichuan Province and Xizang Autonomous Region (Tibet). The river is spanned at Dengke by a metal bridge, one of only three to cross the river in a thousand miles between Batang and Tuotoheyan in the north. Qinghai Province lies to the north. The village is agriculture based and fairly remote, but has become more important in recent years as the bridge across the river is part of a ten year plan to forge a new road link between Sichuan and Lhasa.

I have witnessed many changes to Dengke over the years. On my first visit it took the best part of seven days to reach the village from Chengdu. I shall never forget the first time I travelled the route through Ya'an, Han Yuan, Luding, Kanding, Ganze and Mannigango. Now, with much improved roads, it is possible to arrive in Dengke three days after setting out from Chengdu. I have also noticed a change in the people at Dengke. Gone is the shy curiousness of the villagers. Some ran away from us when we first visited, but that has all changed. We are now not only allowed to visit the hospital but are encouraged to hold clinics there, and conduct surgical operations. We have decorated and rewired the operating theatre, and used it as a base for some of our medical activities. The local people have planted trees to mark our friendship, and we have been able to install solar-powered water systems for the hospital and the Forestry Centre, together with gravity water systems for the village. We are now invited into people's homes and have made many friends.

I have many memories of my visits to Dengke: I recall the couple who spent three days on their horse, to bring their baby boy to our doctors because he was dying; and the accident on the river on my first visit, when a hovercraft hit a huge rock and spun out of control. It was then that I realised how gracious the Tibetan people can be, as they helped us from the stricken craft, fed and watered us, and supplied horses for us to return to Dengke. I also remember, vividly, the journey back. It took seven hours, two of which were in darkness. The horses travelled along a three metre wide track on a ledge half way up the valley wall. I wondered why my horse was walking on the very edge of the precipice, and frightening the life out of me. I was informed later that the horse was a packhorse and walked on the edge to balance the weight he was carrying. If the horse walked too close to the wall, the baggage would strike the wall and throw the horse off balance and over the edge. (I wish the horse had explained that before I set out!)

I remember, too, the feeling of utter helplessness when I went to visit a village about twelve miles away from Dengke, in 1995. It was situated in an idyllic spot at the foot of some mountains, on a rich agricultural plain. It was a beautiful day. The sun was beating down on golden fields of corn, and the summer flowers were in full bloom. This village, which looked like a heavenly place to be, was in fact a leper colony... a place where people were sent to die. We were a party of five—two doctors, two nurses and myself—but there was nothing we could do for any of the people we met.

Space does not permit me to recall all the happy memories experienced at Dengke, but the most unusual was surely being offered a man's wife as a thank you for the help I had given his family! Tibetans are able to marry several wives if they want to, and he obviously thought he could spare one. Now I do not suppose you have ever had an offer like that, but think about it: how would you extricate yourself from that situation without causing offence? It took me two hours!

My expertise is in television production and public relations. I have recorded and produced several documentaries and video promotions reflecting the projects at Dengke. The experiences have had a profound effect on my life, and it has been a privilege to meet and get to understand the Chinese and Tibetan people.

Chapter Nine

June Fish's Story

I am a teacher of hearing and language-impaired people, and an educational audiologist. The long road to Dengke (twice) has stretched many thousands of miles for me, via several unexpected Chinese destinations.

Ever since I discovered the difference between being a nominal Christian and being a *committed* Christian, the voice of God has become clearer and more compelling. When I was a child, my two brothers and I loved the weekends when my parents accommodated visiting speakers, especially those from China. They were fun to be with, and conveyed just enough of their attitudes to life and customs to make us catch some kind of love —and a desire to reach out to disadvantaged people wherever and however God indicated.

To be taken as far away as a remote corner of China/Tibet with no knowledge of the local language in 1995 seemed unthinkable, humanly speaking. I was somewhat disabled. The distance was vast. The roads through the highest mountains were long, dangerous and scary. What could one accomplish in a few weeks? It was another big challenge — a daunting task. But though I felt so inadequate, God gently compelled and enabled.

Over years of dealing with deaf and language-impaired people, I became aware of the importance of non-verbal communication (i.e. apart from formal sign language and printed words.)

In the days when sign language in schools was not accepted, but Scripture was, my class of 8–9 year old profoundly deaf children wanted exciting Bible stories told, acted out and retold. It was then I saw the smile of God reflected in their faces when he triumphed through people such as David, Noah and so many others. One little girl sat, pondered, then uttered: "Ahh! I luff God!" I soon realised I could just step aside and watch God continue. Then most of them wanted a copy of "that book – Holly something" (they meant, of course, the Holy Bible), which I kept on my lap just to keep the facts correct. We saw the same reactions in 1999, beside the Yangtze banks, as our drama group mimed *The Fall, the Tree and the Triumph*. Tibetans had tears in their eyes, with nods of recognition —again, a joy to see the Lord at work, in his way.

I had heard of the hovercraft expedition to the source of the Yangtze, and even hoped to meet the crew when they returned to Hong Kong. I had been doing 'donkey work' there —the nearest chance of visiting inland China after it had been closed for so many years. A big question mark remained in my mind until months later, when two friends casually showed me a video clip of the vast Tibetan mountains where the hovercraft had travelled on its way back from the source. Here it had met its diversion to a burgeoning plan of God. Grounded near a group of friendly, helpful but very needy villagers, the crew were offered packhorses to help them up the riverbank and back to base. Hence friendships began, with far reaching consequences. We still do not know the full impact of this incident. I wanted to learn more, so my two friends promised to keep me posted.

One lazy Saturday morning, I had a phone call to say there was a meeting some hundred miles away at 2 p.m. I dressed, ate half a breakfast, phoned two numbers of unknown people, grabbed my crutches, and met a lift to Loughborough. Arriving on the dot of two o'clock, we were met by Dr Mel Richardson, who greeted me with, "Hello. Are you June? Congratulations, you've passed the first test!"

"What test?" I wondered. I only came to find out how/when/what this amazing hovercraft team had achieved in their daring adventure. I had no intention of joining a team to Base 1. I had left my crutch in the car for the first time in eight months, and walked unaided into the university. I had sustained multiple fractures from an accident the previous summer.

116

Teachers of English were needed. My only offering might have been to share a little advice to future English teachers, which I had tried in a Chinese university in 1992. As a linguistic experimental aid to communication with staff and students in my class, I used some sign language to indicate English verb tense markers, and terms we use which are not found in Chinese. The signs proved more helpful than I had expected.

When Dr Mel heard that I worked with hearing-impaired people he said, "Why not come with us, and do something with deaf people?"

From experience in Africa, and remembering how difficult this could be unless we had the effective equipment and personnel, I said jokingly, "Oh yes, with solar powered hearing aids?" I saw how the engineers had used solar panels for powering water pumps and heating systems. I imagined solar panel headbands linking amplifiers to each ear. We all laughed, except Colin, one far-sighted member who insisted that I should pursue the idea and see what transpired.

I was reluctant, in view of physical limitations, to commit myself to something so huge as an unpredictable expedition in China's high mountain areas, much as the scenery beckoned. My answer to Mel's invitation was one of disinclination to face all the walking in China. He simply replied, "Don't worry, June. We'll get you a horse!" —And he did just that. My fondest memories are of the horse rides—no galloping at hair-raising speeds and losing equipment; more like a donkey ride on a beach —but one on a cliff!

Having been persuaded to join the expedition, I found myself at Chengdu. Waiting for our container of equipment to arrive before our five day bus journey was no occasion to mope around; the opportunity to experience city life was not to be missed. The scene, especially hip-to-hip alongside Chengdu citizens commuting on cycles, was undergoing an interesting process of change. New roads, with or without cycle lanes, were the priority, and buildings came next. They were largely Western-style, but built mostly by hand, and the hardest work was done by female hands. There were holes everywhere along pedestrian ways, plus heaps of rubble to walk or cycle over whilst the rubble clearance in side streets continued. Old Chinese dwellings were fast disappearing, but we could just see signs of ancient lifestyles, which had probably continued for hundreds of years. We were glad to be on our hired bicycles and able to stop and inspect the remains closely.

Then there was an area of preserved and restored fine, elegant buildings. The road back to our hotel base provided much amusement: stern ladies at traffic signals, with a whistle and a red flag to point at the white line. They would fine any cyclist who dared to cross it, even by an inch, at a red light. The tyre pumpers sat on their little seats every few yards; mini stalls on the cycle-lane were selling anything from fruit and vegetables to toothbrushes and underwear. We had to swerve to avoid dragging their wares away. We saw cycle trailers piled high with coal bricks; rickshaws, furniture removal, decorating poles; cycles almost buried in recycle waste, often causing minor collisions. I nearly took a tumble. We all laughed, and pedalled on. No one could tell me what the highway code was for cyclists. I tried hard to guess it, then drew the conclusion that there was an unwritten rule: 'bikes rule. OK?' They would go opposite ways round a roundabout with no obvious 'give way' system. Body language, not hand signals or bells, conveyed a cyclist's intentions —and it worked.

The waiting time was well used during mornings at the hotel. We taught English for two hours to the staff, and then spent a further time learning country dancing together.

On arrival at Dengke, a couple of pack-horses and a trusty guide were made available to take me and one of the doctors to a village, six miles away alongside the Yangtze, under a deep blue sky, with soaring eagles, and yaks for company. There we visited disabled children need-ing advice, and our link man's uncle. I tested his hearing, and gave an appropriate hearing aid, with which he was delighted. He asked for spectacles, but all I could offer was my own pair to try, which he thought were wonderful. Consequently, he changed: now he was ex-cited, and years seemed to fall from his frail demeanour. These Tibetan people had never seen such aids before. On each visit to a patient's house, my Tibetan/Chinese interpreter kindly explained protocol and customs. Food and drink were served before we could get down to business. As we sat round a wooden chest, the lid was taken off an iron bucket-shaped receptacle sunk into the top of the cabinet. This was promptly half filled with brightly-burning coals and covered with a griddle. The huge iron tea kettle was placed on top, ready for the con-stant supply of tea (with yak milk, if desired.) Freshly baked round flat barley loaves and a plate of meat was placed before us. Visitors were expected to carry a rice bowl in their voluminous sleeves, and a sheathed knife in the belt. My interpreter was equipped but I was not, so the best precious china bowls and cups were unwrapped and graciously supplied.

That afternoon, the crowds of patients with hearing problems were waiting in the hospital room assigned to us. The mischievous faces of noisy boys were pressed against the cracked windows. Sights, sounds and smells abounded; it was not an ideal situation for hearing tests! As in the operating theatre next door, we felt like pantomime performers taking three or four times longer than in a normal session-time to get clear results. 'Lord, how can we get the message across kindly?' I sighed, knowing that half the crowd would have to be sent away. Children were given some priority. A little two or three year old girl was brought by her father, who said that she did not respond to sounds and had never uttered any words. When tested, she only responded slightly to a very loud sound given twenty centimetres from one ear. The most powerful hearing aid was selected and gently adjusted to the level she required to discriminate a human voice. After checking with the man holding her on his lap that 'abba' was the Tibetan word for 'daddy', I spoke it through the microphone two or three times. Her face broke into a broad smile and, as the hearing aid microphone was put to her lips, she imitated her first real word, "Abba." Her own daddy was really delighted. I wonder what our Abba has in store for this little girl.

Two ladies were just too deaf to be helped with hearing aids, even to provide the rhythm of sound. Their sadness and pleading pulled at my heart. All I could give was a hug and a blessing, with a desperate attempt to convey my sorrow.

A man showing great strain came on the first visit, in 1995, and when I tried my best Tibetan to ask him his name, he kept saying, "Hamago"; so I wrote it on his record against his name —above his results. A hearing aid really awoke his sociability, and when he also had his sight restored with strong glasses, he went around the locality every day, swinging his umbrella and shouting: "I can hear; I can see!" The new excitement amused everyone.

When the same man appeared four years later, saddened because his hearing aid had broken down, I remembered the face. "Oh!" I said, "I recognise you, your name is Hamago, isn't it?" His two companions laughed in disbelief.

"That's not his name!"

"Why do you laugh?" we asked.

They replied, "'Hamago' means, 'I don't know'!"

Once tested on the audiometer pure tones, a hearing aid could be selected, fitted and set to the best response. In England we often used nonsense words to assess the reception of vowels and consonants. With the Tibetan/Chinese people we could use English words. After certain selected words, I gave them the words 'mechanical diggers', which they found extremely funny. But it released the tension, and we could part on a relaxed note of fun.

The postmistress worked in a little post office, with only a bare wooden counter, bare shelves and two telephone batteries suspended from a couple of wires to a phone which she insisted was broken. So hardly anyone visited her office, except to collect letters which were most infrequent, as many people could not write and had no-one with whom to communicate anyway. Goaga came for a hearing test, and was found to be extremely impaired on the high frequencies. No wonder the telephone seemed dead to her! With an appropriate aid with tone control to boost the high tones, she took on a new lease of life. She could not wait to try the telephone, which worked perfectly well within its limits (maybe to the next town only). "Great, I have a job again!" she exclaimed.

By *Project Dengke 99*, the solar power for hearing aids had developed further. My contacts with a mission school and vocational complex in Botswana opened an opportunity to purchase solar aids with a built-in solar panel. Just four hours in the sun collects enough power for a whole week. Many of the people who received solar aids found it hard to believe, but welcomed a set with delight and very grateful hearts.

There was an old beggar lady with her grandson. Even though they had walked for five days, they had to wait behind those who had walked for even longer. They had received the message of our visit, shouted miles across the mountains —'yodelling' style. After the old lady received her solar aid, I was met again at every corner for a week with her big 'thank you'.

Chapter Ten

Barbara Gunn's Story

My favourite memory of Project Dengke was when a Tibetan lady invited me into her home. The trip to Dengke from Chengdu had been across some bumpy terrain in small, bouncy buses. Our driver would pull out into the direct line of an oncoming truck, slam on his brakes, and then pull in again! On the flat, we learned to live with his overtaking technique, but on steep mountain passes it was a bit hair-raising. Anyway, I have never been great at travelling and I often felt sick. The long days on the bus were tedious, but the scenery was spectacular. We would arrive at a hostel late at night, eat, sleep and leave again early in the morning. A warm welcome was given to us when we arrived at Dengke.

By the time we arrived I had a bad cold, so I had to rest. I was sharing a room with a doctor, a nurse and a midwife; the doctor was able to dispense some antibiotics to me to clear up my cough. I stayed in our compound for a few days. Then, when I felt a bit better, I went for a walk in the village. The men all seemed to be standing around doing nothing. As I walked out of the village, I saw some women washing clothes in the local stream. I wanted a rest, so I sat down beside them. When one lady got up with her washing, she signed for me to follow her; so I followed her into her beautifully carved house. She gave me some yak tea, and made me a dough mixture to eat. I am not sure what we 'talked' about, but she was good fun. At one point, she joked about piercing my ears with a big round earring. When another lady, with children, came in, she signed being pregnant to tell me that this was her daughter. The lady walked back with me to the compound, and I gave her a postcard from my hometown with a picture of a cathedral on it. I wonder if she still has that postcard of Peterborough....

Chapter Eleven

Glyn Davies' Story

I call myself 'Bengda Man', the first Welshman ever to visit the tiny remote village of Bengda, as part of *Project Dengke 99*. It was ROUGH; it was TOUGH; but frontline action 'for Him' always is. For me, it was truly a trip of a lifetime! Verses from Ephesians 2 were given to the team by my mum (now 91+ and a warrior for Jesus in the Congo!), and these were to feature more than once during our trip!

My roles for the expedition were treasurer and administrator. This included: finance, food, translators, vehicles, rotas, procuring jeeps, horse hire, hotel accommodation, walkie talkies, extra bowls for washing up, liaising with officials, negotiation, rotas for devotions, etc., etc. What follows are reminiscences made 'on the road', so you can capture the sense of excitement and awe.

On our arrival at Beijing airport, we found that we had not been booked onto our connecting flight; half the team were to go on separate flights!

We are en route for Kanding — in two coaches (with a bald tyre!) A cemented road is still being made; many workers along the road are mixing cement, using trowels and planks to smooth it out. They then lay dry leaves and sacks over the new surface, to dry it. We now descend to the old rough road, and drive alongside the new one being made! I can only describe the old road as a mud track with potholes, stones, holes, mud, water and rubble.

We stop at a garage. The driver, who has constantly used his horn to warn people of our arrival, buys another horn. (Oh, no!) and places it under the engine! He then fills up with fuel and also fills up the two drums on the top of our bus.

Loos: experience! Gone are the 'sit down' hygienic pans! At least we have a concrete wall separating us from one another. I enter to a dreadful smell, necessitating covering my nose and breathing through a handkerchief! I see a local squatting, and others smoking, and have to copy them! Squatting, I mean. I was glad to get out of there. But that one was to be luxury in comparison with later ones, which we began to mark out of ten!

The scenery is incredible: very lush green. Roadworks: we now experience what is to become the norm for us. We are not allowed to pass until the workers have finished their allotted tasks.

We stop at the driver's village, and also take advantage of another stop.

We have an enforced stop. The spare wheel on our other bus is coming off! We begin climbing, and realise it is getting cooler! We pass more road workers, crushing huge rocks and stones into smaller ones. These are fed onto a conveyor belt, which takes them into a funnel leading to a griddle, and then into a few rollers, which attempt to crush the stones smaller. The machine is similar to a potato cleaner!

Hose pipes are situated at various points along the road. These are used to cool down the overheating brakes of the lorries descending the mountains. Another hold up —for a puncture. On the Erlang Pass. This road has no tarmac, only rocks and mud; there is no overtaking, as we are on a one way system over the mountain pass. If you miss your slot, then the next day the traffic comes from the other direction!

9.45 p.m. We stop again. It is very dark. Only the headlights light up the sky.

We are now in a convoy of traffic —if one breaks down here, we are all stuck. Still climbing….

We have now run out of food, and we are sharing what meagre rations we have. The team is very tired, but in good spirits.

At the side of the bus came these lovely Chinese people, selling pot noodles. They seem to come from nowhere; they have boiling water and pot noodles. This helps feed the ravenous team members!

We are still not on the summit.

The road deteriorates; the vehicles are all over the road; other travellers get quite scared as it becomes very dangerous. It is as well that we are unable to see the big drop at the side of the mountain.

I am still suffering with my jaw —toothache. Kathy, our doctor, manages to get me some antibiotics. Within twenty four hours this helps to heal me, along with the team's prayer. (On my return I find out that the constant pain is the result of a dead nerve being infected in my tooth.)

This is one of the most wonderful and memorable experiences of the whole expedition: Mel guides us up to the church, which is situated about 300 yds up the hill from the hotel where we are staying. We walk along a narrowing street, and view a block of flats undergoing extensive building work, which necessitates copious scaffolding. Chinese ladies are working hard. (They carry heavy loads such as cement, bricks, etc.) The front gate is closed, and so is the heavy front door. A rickety fence at least six feet high is on our right. We enter a little courtyard to hear some singing! We are invited into the dimly lit ante-room by smiling and welcoming Chinese faces, most of whom are ladies. The singing grows louder, and I feel the privilege of being invited into the main room, where others vacate seats to let us sit on stools at the back of the room. This is a square room, with one or two pictures, and Chinese writings which are Scriptures. There is a stove in the middle of the room, and a few pews around the sides are easy chairs, on which elderly ladies and gents are sitting, singing. At the front is a wizened old lady sitting on another comfy chair; an old man is in charge of the music. The singing continues, and I am in awe! I am sitting in the middle of China/Tibet with Christians! They are singing songs which I know in English, so I can join in. We are singing in English, and they in Chinese! Tears begin to spring to my eyes. This indeed is the privilege of a lifetime: to be singing with brothers and sisters in the middle of China! This is awesome. And they are singing: 'He is alive. He is alive; He's alive for evermore!' I just broke down and cried. Jesus is here! I just want to thank the Lord for these people. The singing stops and our translator tells me that they are now reading from John 19. We stand to pray. The sermon lasts for at least forty five minutes. (Reminds me of my mum, who used to preach for ages, it seemed, when I was a little boy. My folks were missionaries in Congo, where I was born.)

[Mel met my parents while in Scotland at a conference. While attending a youth conference, many years ago, he heard my dad speak, and was challenged about World Mission. Years later, I accompany Mel on an expedition!]

On the road again.... 10.30 a.m. We are stopped on a road made of mud, potholes and deep ruts. On our right is a delightful river meandering its way alongside meadows, and in the distance is a town; on our left an embankment, but it opens up to hillside and lovely flowers and greenery. The reason for our stop —an overturned lorry! The driver was negotiating one of the ruts in the road, which necessitated pulling over to the right; however, there is a ravine with a flowing river beneath, and he just did not make it. The lorry is on its left hand side, jammed against a huge wall of earth, with the river on its right. No room to pass. We are stuck. We leave eventually at 7.10 p.m. We suggested that with our expertise we could 'sort' the problem out (i.e. unload the vehicle) and we would be on our way! Not so. The owner had gone to a local village to summon help. He was afraid that if we unloaded, all his goods would be stolen.

More mountains and scenery —this place is so VAST! We are now at the highest mountain: 4850 metres. Our second bus now has a puncture. I had strange feelings in my hands and feet: pins and needles; I am told it is altitude. Even taking our luggage up the stairs I am breathless; this is not usual for me.

Breakfast. I am struggling with it this morning, and would like some familiar food. There are dumplings, and some hot yak milk. On the way to breakfast, I asked Jesus to supply hot milk as I have not had it for a while. And he did!

We finally make it to Dengke —beautiful beyond description. It is as if my role has diminished, now that the various heads of department are fully functional.

I am then asked and encouraged to visit Bengda, where part of our team are exploring possibilities of working. Bengda —nestling among the beautiful, gigantic mountains; the Yangtze flowing majestically down 'Echo Gorge' and the endearing white water of 'Blue Pool'. Bengda is accessed by one road, apart from the many footpaths and horse tracks. Vehicles are rarely seen, except for the occasional lorry carrying the weekly 'goodies'. The odd sound of a tractor pulling a trailer, and the occasional monk on a motorbike or bicycle, breaks the quietness. You arrive from the narrow 300ft mountain road from 'land-slide valley' (only a four-wheel drive vehicle could navigate these roads) —into the scenic vista of Bengda. It has only one shop, which nestles in the wall of the school compound. Locals peer into the darkness and haggle for items. Telephone communication is almost impossible with only one phone in the village. Our accommodation was basic: I was to sleep on a yak matted floor. The room was dusty; no beds; the roof leaked; and we had to rig up a tarpaulin to stop the rain. One light bulb flickered on and off. The office was a small red desk in the cor-ner, with the one and only red phone. Our toilet facility was a small building set in a field. One of its walls was falling down. There were slits in the ground upon which we squatted, and we had a beautiful vista of the surrounding moutains. Our store room was given by the local officials. This was to double up as our kitchen and dining area, plus sleeping quarters for our cook.

Bengda, for me, was to be a meeting place with my God. The others went about their duties and left me all alone as they journeyed on horseback into the mountains to do their work. Apart from my interpreter, I was all alone in the middle of Tibet! I used the time to explore the area and have a refreshing time with God. Isaiah 54:2 gave me strength: 'Enlarge the place of your tent, stretch your curtains wide, do not hold back, lengthen your cords, strengthen your stakes.' So did the song: *You are beautiful beyond description…. Holy God, to whom all praise is due, I stand in awe of you.*

This was a timely meeting with my Lord and God, under a lovely tree, with water running past, the Yangtze, and mountains all around me —to remind me of the Creator; just God ministering to my soul.

I have fallen in love with Dengke and Bengda. Through this ex-perience I was able to return to the team refreshed and ready for 'work'.

We shared a communion service on the banks of the Yangtze. That was another special moment for me. It was such a blessing to see oth-ers receiving medical, educational and building help; and especially working with June Fish, and seeing patients receive their hearing through the solar powered hearing aids that we supplied. We have had many adventures, and more since!

My church has now released me to work for the *Care and Share*

Foundation, so we look forward to the next stage in Dengke. I have since been back, and am so excited about the next chapter of its life, when we shall see the building of the International Friendship Centres.

Chapter Twelve

Keith Richardson's Story

I gestured to the Chinese driver in our lead vehicle to pull over to the side of the road. Both buses in our little convoy rolled to a halt on the dusty track, high up on the winding ascent out of Dengke. "Just give me about ten to fifteen minutes to walk alone up ahead on the road," I said quietly, having already stepped halfway down the metal steps of the front exit door. "It's a good place to stop for a while, and it will give everyone a chance to take some good last photos, looking back into the Yangtze Valley." I set off with quiet determination up the track, savouring the crisp morning air, dodging the occasional potholes and small rocks strewn beneath my feet. A slight breeze murmured through the dark sedge-like grasses along the roadside; a buzzard drifted lazily in the thermals high above. It was the last day of the main *Project Dengke 99*, and the whole team were on their way back to Chengdu: three day's journeying over the high mountain passes, described in one travel guide as some of the most beautiful, and yet dangerous, roads in the world.

Spirits were high among the team, but there was the inevitable mixture of emotions as we contemplated our journey home. There was elation and quiet satisfaction at having achieved worthwhile things, at the same time coupled with a tinge of sadness at leaving the township and the Tibetan people we had got to know in earlier days of the trip.

For most of the team this trip had been an eye–opener, a first-time experience of travelling to a truly remarkable and remote area of the world, of sharing the joys and hardships of journeying, of honing old skills and discovering new talents in the process of seeking to help the people of Dengke and Bengda Townships. Most of all, it had been an opportunity to learn from the local Khamba people themselves, to try to understand a little of their culture, to share some of their hopes and aspirations for the future, and to experience their friendliness and generosity.

For me, it had been an opportunity to return to the area I had last visited some ten years previously. It was in 1989 that I had travelled with a small group of companions as part of a 'recce' for the 1990 British Hovercraft Expedition to the Upper Yangtze. At that time we were almost certainly the first westerners, apart perhaps from a handful of intrepid mountaineers and river-rafters, to visit this part of the Yangtze Valley for probably thirty years. Little did we then realise that Dengke was not only to become the base camp for the Expedition, but would also be the focus of a succession of 'adventures with a purpose' in the years to follow, through the visionary initiatives of the *Care & Share Foundation* co-founded by my elder brother Mel. I should explain that I am a town and land-use planner by training, with a special interest, in recent years, in leisure, recreation, tourism and nature conservation planning, through my experience in the UK as Planning & Development Officer with the Lee Valley Regional Park Authority. Against the further background of my additional skills in the field of outdoor pursuits, including mountaineering, canoeing and wilderness trekking, and considerable experience in researching aid projects for Christian organisations in various parts of the world, Mel had invited me to be part of the *Project Dengke 99* team. My particular role had been to partner John Studley (Agro-forester) and David Rutledge (Outdoor Pursuits Instructor) to investigate opportunities for developing eco-tourism (including outdoor pursuits) and agro-forestry, as a means of stimulating economic growth and alternative employment opportunities for the people of Dengke & Bengda. In these objectives we had been very ably supported by a number of other team members including Suzanne Ewing (architect), Kate Armstrong (botanist), Marc Foggin (field biologist), Paul Lund (photographer), Glyn Davies (Project Administrator) and Philip Chen (Interpreter).

I pressed on purposefully up the track, glancing briefly back to see that the rest of the team had clambered out of the buses and were clustered around in small groups, admiring the view of the magnificent valley with far glimpses of scattered buildings on the outskirts of Dengke. The morning sun glimmered softly on the Yangtze winding its way like a tiny silver ribbon in the distance. I had something to do which had been on my mind for several days: a task to perform, which would lay to rest a yearning in my heart that had been there since I last visited this amazingly beautiful part of the high Tibetan plateau ten years before.

It was on a similar day to this, clear and bright, with feathery clouds brushing the mountain tops, that the previous Hovercraft Expedition recce team had arrived at the head of the valley, back in 1989. We had driven solidly for nine hours a day for three and a half days from Chengdu, adventured our way over three sixteen thousand feet mountain passes, including the mighty Erlang, up through the forests and snowline, and descended again. We were tired and hungry, but eagerly awaited our first glimpse of the mighty Yangtze. Suddenly there it was, the great river itself, just a bright thread weaving its course to the north of the valley. "Let's stop here for a while," I had said. "It would be good to rest awhile, and record our first sight of the River: perhaps we could build a little cairn by the roadside? And we can also offer a prayer of thanks to God for bringing us safely here." Within a few minutes we had built our little cairn (not a masterpiece of engineering, just small boulders piled as neatly as possible), to be a reminder in that place; and we prayed to the Lord. We were thankful to our Heavenly Father for bringing us safely to the end of that part of the journey, and felt optimistic about new opportunities and discoveries that awaited us high on the Tibetan Plateau.

I strode on steadily up the track, taking in occasional deep breaths of the thin, clean mountain air, thankful that I had already become adjusted to the high altitude. By now, the rest of the Project Dengke team were well in the distance. I rounded a little rocky bluff by the side of the road leading to a wide stony plateau, punctuated by clumps of spiky grass and occasional larger, moss-covered boulders. A golden furred mammal, the size of a large rabbit but without the long ears, scurried off for the safety of its burrow further up the track, clearly startled by my sudden appearance.

I could no longer see the two team buses, since the track dropped away steeply at this point, but here was a commanding view over the rest of the valley. This was the place where, I was sure, my companions and I had built the little 'cairn of thanks' all those years before. There was little trace of the structure now: the ravages of the intervening years of harsh winter storms, wind, rain and snowfall had, no doubt, swept aside the small pile of stones. What better place, I thought, to build another cairn, and once again give thanks on behalf of the team to a loving Heavenly Father, who had watched over the events of the previous weeks since we had arrived in China, and had blessed, guided, encouraged and sometimes even disciplined us, as we had sought to demonstrate care and concern for the people of Dengke and Bengda? The simple expression of thankfulness had an even greater personal significance for me. There had been a time when I thought I should never again have the opportunity to return to this fascinating and incredibly beautiful part of the world. I had suffered a period of severely debilitating nervous illness in the months following my return from China in 1989; and, as a result, I had missed out on part of the ambition of a lifetime: to join my brother, Mel, and other members of the British Hovercraft Expedition, a year later, on their unique journey, described so vividly in Dick Bell's book, *To the Source of the Yangtze*. It is hard to describe the level of pain and frustration that I had felt at that time, and the difficult few months that were subsequently experienced by my family as I struggled back to full health. My dear late wife, Joan, as always, had been a tremendous source of prayerful support and encouragement as I had first travelled to China and planned for the main expedition over several years. She had desperately wanted me to get back to Dengke, and had been so disappointed when I could not make it. I had come to stand firmly in my Christian belief, however, that the things we experienced in those dark days finally served to open us to more of God's blessing, and that we were strengthened as a family.

Aware that quite soon the two team buses would be starting their way up the pass again, I resolutely set about gathering some small rocks from the roadside verge. As I knelt to lay the first stones in place, I could not help recalling some of the experiences of the previous two weeks. Memories flooded back of the first trip in Marc Foggin's jeep up the Yangtze Valley, some fifty kilometers from Dengke up to Bengda Township. It had been a pioneering trip, since none of the team had travelled the road before. Mel, as overall project team leader, had understandably expressed his concerns about the safety of team members travelling over unknown terrain and had looked to Marc, Peter Gunner and myself for some initial assessment of the road conditions. It had been an exciting and fascinating first recce, to say the least. I recalled the crossing of a swift-flowing local tributary, the vehicle up to its wheel arches, with Marc drawing upon all his driving skills as he edged and bumped his sturdy Chinese-made vehicle over the treacherously slippery, boulder-strewn river bed, with engine revving hard. I visualised our cautious and steady progress on the sometimes narrow and eroded track high above the east bank of the Yangtze, with spectacular views over sections of rapids and the final approaches into Bengda Township.

Following another recce by other team members, it was a few days later that our eco-tourism and agro-forestry study team had 'set up camp' in some semi-derelict buildings forming part of the compound of the District Secretary, who had been waiting to receive us. This was no luxury accommodation, and neither did we expect it; just straw-filled mattresses on an earth floor on which to lay our sleeping bags, and washing facilities comprising tin bowls with water provided from a nearby stream. But we were happy enough to have a reasonably waterproof roof over our heads, and a base from which to conduct our surveys, not to mention the services of our own Chinese cook, who had travelled with the group up from Dengke.

Understandably, the local people had been, initially, a little cautious about these strange foreigners who had appeared in their midst. Soon, however, we had become the centre of friendly attention, and won the trust and confidence of the District Secretary and inhabitants of the five or so little hamlets that made up the population of Bengda Township, greatly aided by the communication skills of team member Philip Chen and a locally recruited Tibetan interpreter. I fondly recalled the privilege of being invited into the homes of many of the villagers, experiencing their friendly welcome, gaining new insights into their culture and daily lives, sharing something of their dreams and aspirations, and laughing, over countless cups of green tea. Then there was the spectacularly colourful dancing display, which had been specially arranged in honour of the team at Bengda. I smile inwardly as I remember John Studley, Paul Lund, Rob Alcock and myself drawing much amusement from the villagers, as we accepted an invitation to take part in the dancing.

My little cairn was taking shape now. Across the valley I could just make out some distant figures of mounted horsemen trotting along one of the precariously narrow paths on the steep hillside. It brought back happy memories of the time I had trekked with a sturdy little Tibetan pony up into the Luoxu Nature Reserve; of hours spent in a hard wooden saddle, with other team members, up in the high passes; of the spectacular scenery, the hillsides covered in wild flowers; of lammergeier (Bearded Vulture) circling and swooping in the thin mountain air; of sleeping outside under the stars, and waking with a dusting of frost on my bivvy bag.

Something caught my attention. I looked round to discover, to my surprise, that I was not alone at the top of the pass. Standing only some twenty yards away was the lone figure of a young Tibetan man. Dressed in the long, dark red robes of a monk, and wearing a traditional Tibetan, wide-brimmed hat, I surmised that he must have been standing watching me for some time, no doubt intensely curious to know what this foreigner was doing alone at the side of the track. I beckoned for him to come over, to which he gladly responded. The Tibetan clearly understood no English and I spoke only a few words of local Khamba dialect. I gestured with my hand to confirm that I was intending to add more stones to the pile; he smiled and, to my delight, immediately responded by gathering some rocks himself and placing them on the structure.

I had one last little task to carry out. Reaching into my jacket pocket, I searched for a while amongst a bundle of papers, until I found what I was looking for. It was a copy of a photograph of Joan and myself, taken some six years previously —after my own illness, but just before she was diagnosed with terminal cancer. Joan had a living faith in the resurrection of our Lord Jesus Christ from the dead, as I have; and I know, as Joan knew, that we shall be with him in heaven for ever.

I showed the picture briefly to my new found friend, placed it down between the rocks of the cairn, and added the last couple of stones. The significance of my action did not seem lost on the Tibetan man. I placed my hand on his shoulder and said a brief prayer for him that, somehow, God would reveal to him the real truth of salvation in Jesus Christ, the only one who gives true hope, joy and peace. On

behalf of the team, I also thanked our Heavenly Father for all his goodness in meeting our needs, and for allowing me to fulfil my ambition
to return to this beautiful valley; and I prayed for future blessings on
the people of Dengke and Bengda.

I felt that this little episode had taken on a meaning that even I
could not have anticipated when I had requested the opportunity for
some time alone at the head of the track. It brought to mind the on-
going partnership that was being built between the people of Dengke
and teams from the *Care & Share Foundation*; the Lord was reminding
us that we must commit our talents, skills and ambitions to him, for
it is only in his strength and by his blessing that any lasting work will
be achieved for his glory.

The low growl of diesel engines labouring round the sweeping
bend of the track heralded the arrival of the team buses. Waving goodbye to my Tibetan friend, I clambered back on board the lead vehicle.
With a swish of hydraulics, the bus door closed behind me, and in seconds we had continued on our way. Our bus swayed and bumped
around another tight corner of the track, and the view of the Yangtze
Valley and Dengke was suddenly gone. I sank down into my seat,
closed my eyes and reflected on how long it might be before any of us
might have the privilege of returning for further adventures in this remarkable valley 'nearest the sun'.

Appendix A

Some Local Customs

One of the great joys of Project Dengke has been befriending local people. Philip, one of our interpreters, hails from a town similar to Dengke and we have summarised some of his comments here.

Housing

Traditionally, Tibetans build their houses with very small windows and complicated designs, using the same materials as the Han Chinese. Living rooms have a special layout, consisting of a low set of desks, tables and seats placed on a carpeted floor specifically facing the direction of other furniture fixtures. Honoured guests and senior people sit on these chairs as a sign of respect. Children usually sit very low on the floor, far away from those of higher rank.

Language.

In my hometown, although the language is completely different from Tibetan, it can be written or pronounced using Tibetan letters. Only about five or six thousand people speak it, and a lot of Chinese words are incorporated, such as the days of the week. My friends speak both Chinese and the local language quite fluently, but the children living among the Tibetan people do not usually speak Mandarin until they have reached school age. So sometimes a local teacher is employed to teach the children both languages.

Costume

Our local Tibetan costume is somewhat similar to that of the Chung nationalities, though the hats are different. Whilst both men and women have their own dress styles, it is now only the women and older men who are likely to wear their traditional costumes. The designs are quite simple, and have very little artistic merit in my opinion. The Han people in my hometown, though, dress in the same way as other Chinese people.

Marriage

Marriage customs for both the local Tibetan and Han Chinese people are now almost identical. Traditionally, Tibetan people were engaged very young, by their parents, and then married when they grew up. They had no choice. Now things have changed and they can marry whoever they like.

Nonetheless, in TAR itself, the old rituals of proposal, engagement and marriage are still widely adhered to. Family marriage contracts can include the use of poems, if they involve inheritance details. The day before the wedding, the bridegroom sends the bride fine gifts. His mounted representative, accompanied by a retinue, fetches the bride on the wedding day itself.

[An interesting insight into how girls can unofficially make their feelings known to eligible bachelors was provided in one of the earlier expeditions. A girl dropped some pebbles into the lap of an unsuspecting team member sitting in a jeep.

He found out some weeks later this traditionally means he is invited to return to her house late at night to lob the pebbles up to her window and ask her out. Nice as she was, he declined.]

Eating, drinking and dancing

The local Han people of my town cook wonderful meals, involving a wide variety of dishes for each meal. However, the Tibetan people live very simply. They drink butter tea and eat tsampa, which is a traditional kind of Tibetan food, and enjoy singing, dancing —and drinking!

Appendix B

Songs, blues and dubious compositions composed in Dengke

DENGKE LOO SONG

Well I woke up this morning
Radio China in my head
Cockroaches in my sleeping bag
And pains inside my head
I've got the Dengke Blues
I've got the Dengke Blues...Real Bad
The cooking's pretty good
But the latrines they're... Real Bad

Way down in Tin Pan Alley
Crouching in trap number three
Went in there with my toilet bag
But it didn't come out with me
I've got the Dengke Blues
I've got the Dengke Blues...Real Bad
The Cook's very able
But the toilets.....they make me sad

Spoke to my mother
On satellite telephone
Said, "Momma I've got the blues real bad
I just wanna get home"
I've got the Dengke Blues
I've got the Dengke Blues...Real Bad
Tasted good when we ate it
But it can make you bad

NEAREST THE SUN

Well I woke up this morning
Urg..................
Urg..................
Urg..................
I've got the Dengke Blues
I've got the Dengke Blues...Real Bad
It's OK in here
But the toilets..............

I went down one evening
To a Karaoke Bar
If this is entertainment
Man I wish I had a car
I've got the Dengke Blues
I've got the Dengke Blues...Real Bad
If you think the singing's bad
Just try and shift us

We're on the team together
We thought it would be fun
But by the time we got to Dengke
We are grateful for a bun
We've got the Dengke Blues
We've got the Dengke Blues...Real Bad
Walking's pretty good
But driving drives me mad

FIXED PRICE CONTRACT

Some say it's their birthday
But we know it's a lie
They're trying to get some Mars bars
English pigs will fly
There's cabbage now for breakfast
For dinner and for tea
If I never see a yak again
It's still too soon for me

They say a picnic horse ride
Is planned with lots of food
But things turned out quite differently
We just weren't in the mood
We all got hypothermia
And mud up to our ears
But Mel he had a cunning plan
And said, "The buck stops here"

They said they'd get a bus for us
We knew it was all talk
Bumping along those mountain roads
Be quicker if we walked
Through another village
I hope were in for tea
We're "on a fixed price contract"....

We're happy here in Dengke
We've had a real good time
We'll miss the Yangtze River
And the Karaoke rhymes
We love to sing like Elvis
And dance with Mr Lee
We're "on a fixed price contract"
That costs no FEC*

"Change your money?"

*local money

BUNS, BUNS, GLORIOUS BUNS

A Lecturer from Loughborough
Was standing one day,
On the banks of the turbulent Yangtze;
He stared at the bottom
As he pondered a way
To invent a renewable energy;
When high in the sky,
Came beaming right down,
A golden bright ray of the sun.

A Lecturer from Loughborough
Was not such a duffborough;
He packed his great fiddle and sun;
Sun, sun, glorious sun,
Nothing quite like it to make water run;
So follow me, follow,
Down to the River;
There we shall tap Dengke's glorious sun

So in 1992 they all came together,
Mel and his motley crew;
Heavy John Whatmore and RMB Sneller
Hiding beneath an umbrella;
Believing their word its true;
By doctors who all became ill;
Aided by Gunners and several others,
What do you think they all ate?
Buns, buns glorious buns,
Nothing quite like it for giving the runs;
So follow me, follow, down to the floodlights,
And there we shall swallow
Those heavy steam buns....
Etc., etc.

KANGDING LOO SONG

My, my, loo has got no door
And you just want to squat there
Make a visit everyday
But the smell is a nightmare
Waan, waan
My, my, loo will change you

Words by Bobby Graham.
Black Panther is one of the biggest rock groups in China.
After a 'chance' meeting with Mel Richardson at Chengdu airport they recorded
a special tribute song as their expression of support.
The song is available on the web:
http://www.mech.port.ac.uk/zyz/public_html/dengke/song.html
or http://www.projectdengke.com

THERE'S A WAY

I HEARD A CRY FROM THE PURPLE MOUNTAINS
IT COMES FROM PEOPLE WHO HAVE LOST THE PATH TO LIFE
CRYING OUT TO FEEL SOME CARING
REACHING OUT TO TOUCH SOME SHARING
THEIR WORLD IS GREY AND FULL OF STRIFE

I HEARD A SIGH FROM THE MISTY FORESTS
IT SEEMED TO CRY OUT TO THE UNFORGIVING DAY
IT'S A LIFE OF NO ONE CARING
IT'S A LIFE OF NO ONE SHARING
A LIFE THAT SLOWLY WASTES AWAY

AS WE IGNORE THEM THE CHILDREN DIE IN FEAR
WE CANNOT LEAVE THEM TO DROWN IN THEIR OWN TEARS
SO LET US HELP THEM. HELP THEM TO BREAK CLEAR
FROM THE LIFE THAT ENGULFS THEM,
TO A LIFE THAT'S BRIGHT AND CLEAR

LISTEN TO ME, THERE'S A WAY IF YOU WANT TO FIND IT
OPEN MINDS AND CARING HEARTS ARE YOURS TO SEE
THEN YOU WILL FIND
THERE'S A WEALTH OF HOPE AWAITING
GIVE US TIME, FOR WE HAVE COME TO SET YOU FREE

(STRING SECTION)

I FELT THE TOUCH OF AN OLD MAN'S ANGUISH
I'VE BRUSHED THE TEARS OF PAIN AND GRIEF FROM A
CHILD'S FACE

NEAREST THE SUN

NOW'S THE TIME TO CHANGE TO SMILES
ALL THE FEAR THAT'S SEEN FOR MILES
TO BRING TO YOU ALL, THE GIFT OF FAITH

AS WE IGNORE THEM THE CHILDREN DIE IN FEAR
WE CANNOT LEAVE THEM TO DROWN IN THEIR OWN TEARS
SO LET US HELP THEM. HELP THEM TO BREAK CLEAR
FROM THE LIFE THAT ENGULFS THEM
TO A LIFE THAT'S BRIGHT AND CLEAR

(GROUP BREAK)

LISTEN TO ME, THERE'S A WAY IF YOU WANT TO FIND IT
OPEN MINDS AND CARING HEARTS ARE YOURS TO SEE
THEN YOU WILL FIND
THERE'S A WEALTH OF HOPE AWAITING
GIVE US TIME, FOR WE ARE HERE TO SET YOU FREE.
LISTEN TO ME, AND BELIEVE THAT WE CARE ABOUT YOU
DON'T YOU CRY NO MORE,
WE CAN HELP YOU CHANGE YOUR LIFE

(GUITAR SOLO)

LISTEN TO ME, THERE'S A WAY IF YOU WANT TO FIND IT
OPEN MINDS AND CARING HEARTS ARE YOURS TO SEE
THEN YOU WILL FIND, THERE'S A WEALTH OF
HOPE AWAITING
GIVE US TIME, FOR WE ARE HERE TO SET YOU FREE.
(REPEAT) GIVE US TIME, FOR WE ARE HERE TO SET YOU FREE.

© *Bobby Graham Music. Used by permission*

Appendix D
Kangding Love Song (Kangding Ching Ge)

This is a very famous traditional love song in Kangding. People get together on Pau Ma (Horse Racing) Mountain every year where horse racing is a local festival. Young men use the opportunity to court their girl friends and sing songs of love. It is available on the web:

http://www.geocities.com/john_f_studley/Kanding.htm

or

http://www.projectdengke.com

1.   pau ma / liu liude/ sha-an shang
      yi door / liu liude / yuin your
      duan duan / liu liude / zhau-zai
      Kangding / liu liude / cheng your
      yue liang / wan / wan
      Kangding / liu liude / cheng your.

A running horse, slipping and sliding on the mountain
A single cloud shines directly upon the Kangding city wall
The moon's a crescent, it shines directly upon the Kangding city wall

2.   lee jia / liu liude / da-jie
      ren chai / liu liude / how your
      zhang jia / liu liude / da-ger
      kan shang / liu liude / ta your
      yue liang / wan / wan
      kan shang / liu liude / ta your

The Li family's eldest daughter had fine talents
The Zhang family's eldest son took a fancy to her
The moon's a crescent, he took a fancy to her

3.   yi lai /liu liude / kan-shang
      ren chai / liu liude / how your
      er lai / liu liude / kan-shang
      hui dang / liu liude / jia your
      yue liang / wan / wan
      hui dang / liu liude / jia your

The first thing he noticed was her fine talents
The second thing he noticed was she could run a household
The moon's a crescent, she could run a household

4.   shi jian / liu liude / newi-zer
      ren ni / liu liude / ai your
      shi jian / liu liude / lan-zer
      ren ni / liu liude / chew your
      yue liang / wan / wan
      ren ni / liu liude / chew your

The girls of the world are there for you to pursue
The boys of the world are there for you to love
The moon's a crescent, they're there for you to love

SICHUAN/TIBETAN CHINESE RECIPES

[Publisher's Disclaimer: Please note that we have not tested the following recipes, and so cannot be held responsible for the results! They are printed in good faith as received, solely for academic reference.]

1.   **CHENGDU SIZZLING RICE WITH SHRIMPS
        AND TOMATO SAUCE
        CHENGDU XIA REN ROU PIAN (GUOBA)**

This simple, tasty and delightfully 'noisy' dish owes its origins to the traditional way that rice is cooked in many Sichuan households. When rice sticks to the bottom of their large round copper pots it is removed, roasted over a slow fire and then used again. These slabs of reheated, crispy rice, called 'guoba', make a delicious sizzling meal when boiling sauce is poured over them. The alternative name of 'Thunderbolt out of the blue' is very appropriate!

General Ingredients:
225g (approx. 8oz) raw peeled shrimps
Groundnut or corn oil for deep frying
400g (approx. 14oz) chopped canned tomatoes
2.5ml (approx. 1/4 tsp) salt
2.5ml (approx. 1/4 tsp) sugar
10ml (approx. 2 tsp) thin soy sauce
15ml (approx. 3 tsp) Shaohsing wine or medium dry sherry
450ml (approx. 16 fl. oz) clear stock
30ml (approx. 6 tsp) cornflour dissolved in 60ml (approx. 12 tsp) clear stock or water
12 pieces of 'guoba'

'Guoba' Ingredients:
400g (approx.14oz) cooked rice
30ml (approx.6 tsp) groundnut or corn oil

Marinade Ingredients:
2.5ml (approx. 1/4 tsp) salt
10ml (approx. 2 tsp) cornflour
1/2 egg white

Method:
1. Prepare the Guoba
Loosen the cooked rice and leave to dry for 4 hrs. Form the rice into 'biscuits' and place on baking trays lightly brushed with oil. Roast for 20 mins (or until

brown) on the top shelf of a pre-heated oven at 220C (425F gas mark 7), then cool and and store in an airtight container.

2. Prepare the Marinade.

Add salt, cornflour and egg white to the shrimps in a bowl. Stir to coat evenly and marinade in a fridge for at least 3hrs.

3. Cooking

Lightly deep fry the shrimps for 30 secs in a wok or frying pan (until almost cooked or pinkish). Remove shrimps, strain and keep close by. Preheat two casserole table dishes at about 140C (275F gas mark 1) i.e. one for the sizzling rice and one for the sauce. Place chopped tomatoes, salt, sugar, soy sauce, wine or sherry, and stock in a saucepan and bring slowly almost to the boil. Reduce heat and stir in the dissolved cornflour and leave over a low flame or on a hot plate. Reheat the oil to 190C (375F) or until a cube of stale bread browns in 50secs. Add the 'gouba' and deep fry for 2 mins or until golden brown. Place in one of the hot casserole serving dishes and keep in oven. Add shrimps to the tomato sauce and bring to a fast boil, and then place in the other hot casserole dish.

Serving:

Place the 'guoba' dish on the table and pour the sauce into it. Serve portions as soon as the 'sizzling' subsides.

2. **SICHUAN GAN BIAN (STIR-FRIED) BEEF STICKS SICHUAN GAN BIAN NIU ROU SI**

The practice of stir frying in a wok (known in China as a 'guo') owes its origins to the lack of wood and fuel in certain areas. Tinder wood and straw tends to flare up quickly and so a cooking pan with a large surface area was developed to evenly distribute and capture the maximum amount of heat in the shortest period of time. A typical city family in Chengdu today would cook over two small gas rings.

Ingredients:

500g (approx. 1lb) beef
20g (approx. 3/4oz) tender root ginger
50g (approx. 10 tsp) rice wine or sherry
400g (approx. 14oz) celery
2 roasted peppercorns (or 1 chilli with stalk removed)
50g (approx. 10 tsp) thick broad-bean/pepper sauce
3g (approx. 1/2 tsp) salt
80g (approx. 16 tsp) rape seed oil
3g (approx. 1/2 tsp) Chinese prickly ash (optional)

Preparation:

Beef: cut into 8–10cm (3–4in) 'chopsticks'

Celery: trim and cut into 5cm (2in) sticks
Ginger and peppercorns: cut into fine slices
Thick broadbean/pepper sauce: ensure beans and peppers are well chopped
Method:
Fry peppercorns in a wok for 75 secs and remove and set on one side
Add beef sticks and let water evaporate
Add rice wine or sherry, ginger slices, thick broadbean/pepper sauce, and fry
the beef sticks until no further steam emerges. Add peppercorns again then stir
in celery and salt. Transfer to a hot serving dish and cover with Chinese prickly
ash (optional).

3.   **BRAISED HAM WITH PEAS**
      HUO TUI GING YUN
Similar to Western braising, this cooking technique is often used after initial
stir frying. Sauces can be thickened at the end of the process.
Ingredients:
500g (approx. 1lb) fresh shelled peas
100g (approx. 1/4 lb) ham
50g (approx. 2oz) lard
4g (approx. 3/4 tsp) salt
750g (approx. 27 fl. oz)) chicken soup or stock
75g (approx.2.7 fl. oz) starch fluid
Method:
Heat lard in a saucepan for 70 secs, add ham and stir for 30 secs, add peas and
stir for a further 30 secs. Pour soup into the mix, add salt, then cook for 30
mins. Mix in starch fluid, stir, then serve.

4.   **SICHUAN GONGBAO (DEEP-FRIED) CHICKEN CUBE**
      SICHUAN GONG BAO JI DING
The wok, though traditionally used for stir frying, can also be used for deep
frying. Although pork is the most widely eaten meat throughout China (in fact
the Chinese word for meat literally partly translates as pork) chicken and duck
must run as a close second. Live chickens in the market places of Chengdu and
Sichuan are commonplace and a very popular buy with shoppers.
Ingredients:
250g (approx 1/2 lb) chicken
4 roasted peppercorns
20g (approx. 1 oz) root ginger
75g (approx. 2.7 fl oz) rape seed oil
2 garlic cloves

15g (approx. 3/4 oz) green onions
5g (approx 1 tsp) white sugar
1.5g (1/4 tsp) salt
5g (approx.1 tsp) vinegar
20g (approx. 4 tsp) soybean sauce
50g (approx. 1.5 oz) roasted peanut kernels
75g (approx. 2.7 fl oz) starch fluid

Preparation:

Beat chicken with the blunt edge of a knife and cut into 1.5 cm (1/2 in) cubes. Mix starch with water to make starch fluid. Mix chicken cubes with the starch fluid, salt, sugar and vinegar. Cut green onions into small pieces, shred the garlic and ginger, and cut the peppercorns into rings.

Cooking Method:

Heat the oil in a wok until hot, fry the peppercorns until they change colour. Add the chicken cubes, stir constantly for 5 mins, add ginger, garlic and green onions. Mix the peanut kernels with the chicken cubes and quickly toss in the pan. Serve in pre-heated hot dish

5.   **CHENGDU STEAMED BEEF SHREDS IN RICE POWDER CHENGDU FEN ZHENG NIU ROU**

Typically, a Chinese 'steamer' consists of bamboo strips made into circular 'sieves' stacked up to five high above a wok or pan containing boiling water. A form of inverted wok can be placed on top as a lid. Woks with a lid and trivet can also be used. Charming in appearance, it is not uncommon for bamboo steamers and contents to be centrepieces on the serving table.

Ingredients:

500g (approx. 1 lb) beef
2.5g (approx. 1/2 tsp) salt
30g (approx. 6 tsp) soybean sauce
2g (approx. 1/2 tsp) Chinese prickly ash
25g (approx. 5 tsp) rice wine or sherry
100g (approx. 20tsp) coarse rice powder (not fine ground)
30g (approx. 6 tsp) thick broad-bean pepper sauce
25g (approx. 3/4 oz) green onions
3g (approx. 3/4 tsp) ginger
10g (approx. 2 tsp) sugar
50g (approx. 10 tsp) rape seed oil
50g (approx. 1.5 oz) celery leaves or parsley
50g (approx. 10 tsp) chicken stock or soup

Method:

Cut beef into 2.5cm (1 in) shreds. Chop the green onions and ginger. Mix the salt, soybean sauce, ginger, green onions, Chinese prickly ash, sugar, rice wine or sherry, and rape seed oil into a small amount of soup (50g). Soak the beef shreds in the mixture, mix with coarse rice powder, place in a pan. Steam for 30 mins and serve in a dish garnished with celery leaves

6. **KANGDING TOMATO AND EGG FLOWER SOUP**
   KANGDING FAN GIE DAN HUA TANG

This is a very common 'every day' soup dish in Sichuan. Soups are invariably served at the end of a meal (or between courses) and are more likely to be thin and clear (albeit with food floating in them), rather than thick and stodgy.

Ingredients:
500g (approx.1 lb) tomatoes
2 eggs
4g (approx. 3/4 tsp) salt
750g (aprox. 27 fl oz) water
1 tsp butter
25g (approx. 3/4 oz) green onions (cut into 1 cm sticks)

Method:
Quickly boil the water. Beat the eggs and slice the tomatoes. Put the tomato slices and butter into the boiling water. Pour in the beaten eggs once the water is boiling again and stir. Add the salt and chopped onions. Serve hot

7. **YU XIANG AUBERGINES**
   YU XIANG GIE ZI

'Yu xiang' means 'fragrantly smelling of fish' (even though it is not in the ingredients) and is a special favourite in Sichuan.

Ingredients:
500g (approx. 1 lb) aubergines (stalks removed)
20g (approx. 3/4 oz) root ginger
20g (approx. 3/4 oz) garlic
30g (approx 1 oz) green onions
30g (approx. 1 oz) pickled chilli
1g (approx. 1/4 tsp) salt
30g (approx. 6 tsps) soybean sauce
20g (approx. 4 tsps) sugar
20g (approx. 4 tsps) vinegar
50g (approx. 10 tsps) rape seed oil
50g (approx. 10 taps) starch fluid
300g (approx. 11 fl oz) chicken soup or stock

Preparation:

Cut aubergines length-ways, separate into two halves, then cut cross-ways.
Chop the ginger and garlic into fine pieces (grain size).
Slice the the green onions and pickled chilli into rings
Method:
Heat the oil in a wok and add aubergine pieces and stir. Add pickled chilli,
soybean sauce, salt, ginger, garlic, soup, and cook for 2 mins. Add green on-
ions, sugar, starch fluid and stir. Add vinegar and serve

8.   **MA PO BEANCURD**
       MA PO DOU FU

'Mapo' is the nickname of an old lady in Chengdu who first created this spicy
dish around the turn of the century in the Qing dynasty.

Ingredients:
500g (approx. 1 lb) beancurd
100g (approx. 3 oz) beef, very finely chopped
75g (approx. 15 tsps) rape seed oil
50g (approx. 10 tsps) thick broad-bean/pepper
1.5g (approx. 1/4 tsp) salt
75g (approx. 3 oz) garlic bolts (sprouts) or green onions
25g (approx. 5 tsps) soybean sauce
20g (approx. 2/3 oz) ground pepper
400g (approx. 14 fl oz) meat soup
4 tablespoons starch fluid
1 pinch Chinese prickly ash
1 tsp ground chilli
Method:
Cut the beancurd into 2.5cm (1 in) cubes and soak it in boiling water for 2
mins to rid it of any astringent tastes and set on one side. Cut the garlic bolts
or green onions into 2.5cm (1 in) sticks. Heat the oil for 1 min, add beef, let
water evaporate. Add broad-bean pepper sauce and ground chilli; heat until
the oil turns red. Add salt, soybean sauce, meat soup, and cook for 3 mins
gently stirring and adding the beancurd Add garlic bolts (or green onions) and
starch fluid. Sprinkle Chinese prickly ash on top of the dish and serve.

Appendix F

PROJECT DENGKE TEAM MEMBERS 1992–2002

China/Tibet team members are listed alphabetically below. Many other vital members were involved in support across the world and are listed elsewhere.

Dr	Robin ALCOCK	Dr	Phillip AMBLER
Mrs	Geralyn ANDERSON	Mr	Peter ANDERSON
Miss	Kathleen ARMSTRONG	Miss	Janet BAAIJENS
Mr	Richard BARLOW	Dr	Arne BRANTSAETER
Mrs	Madalyn BROOKS	Mr	Sam BROOKS
Dr	John BURSLEM	Mr	Tim CHAPMAN
Miss	Helen CHIA	Dr	Gareth CLEGG
Mr	Roger COOKE	Mr	Peter COULSON
Ms	Ao-Li DAI	Mr	Glyn DAVIES
Mr	Leslie DENNIS	Miss	Maria DIFINIZIO
Mr	Laurence EAST	Mr	Steven ELLARD
Mr	Robin EVANS	Miss	Suzanne EWING
Miss	Helen FARRINGTON	Miss	June FISH
Dr	Marc FOGGIN	Miss	Barbara FORBES
Mr	Grant FREEMAN	Dr	Colin GARNER
Mr	Stuart GERRISH	Mrs	Rosamund GERRISH
Mrs	Jill GIBSON	Mr	Patrick GLEAVE
Mr	Paul GLENDENNING	Dr	Frank GREEN
Mr	James GREENER	Miss	Barbara GUNN
Mr	Jonathan GUNNER	Miss	Hazel GUNNER
Mr	Peter GUNNER	Miss	Reidun HAUGEN
Mr	Andre HEAD	Mr	Keith HOPPER
Dr	Kevin ILSLEY	Rev	Steven KEMPTON
Mrs	Helen KEMPTON	Mr	Niels KOFOED
Dr	Tim LAVY	Dr	Wei Shen LIM
Mr	Steve LOWE	Mr	Paul LUND
Mr	Ang LUO	Miss	Andrea LUSK
Miss	Jennifer MACHARDY	Dr	Jim MARPLE
Mrs	Christine MARTIN	Dr	Jon MARTIN
Miss	Lucy MAUNSELL	Miss	Kirsty MCBETH
Dr	Steve MITCHELL	Miss	Katie NEWTON
Mr	John OWENS	Mr	Jeremy PECK
Dr	Rachel PINNIGER	Ms	Vera POOLEY
Mr	Mike PRITCHARD	Mr	Keith RICHARDSON
Prof.	Mel RICHARDSON	Mr	Bob RIDEOUT

Mr	David RUTLEDGE		Mrs	Sheila SHARPLES
Mr	Jack SHARPLES		Miss	Nicky SHAW-HAMILTON
Mr	Martin SKINNER		Dr	Kathy SMITH
Mr	Andrew SNELLER		Mrs	Pia STEENHAM
Mr	Klaas STEENHAM		Dr	John STUDLEY
Miss	Morna TAN		Miss	Val THOMPSON
Dr	Marion TORRANCE		Mrs	Sandra WATSON
Capt.	Rob WATSON		Mr	John WHATMORE
Dr	Michael WISHEART			

Appendix G

PROJECT DENGKE SPONSORS 1992–2002
Note: Individual sponsors are listed elsewhere

3M Health Care Ltd
Alitalia Airline Ltd
Beautrice Laing Trust
Black Panther Chinese Rock Band
Blue Meanies Beatles Tribute Band
Boddingtons Ltd
British Steel plc
Care and Share Foundation
Casio Ltd
Charles Hall (Hosiery) Ltd
China Trading Associates (CTA) Ltd
Ciba Geigy Adhesives Ltd
Clarks Shoes
Federal Emergency Management Agency USA
G Harman Evangelical Trust
Herbert Pool Ltd
Hilden Charitable Trust

Continued overleaf

PROJECT DENGKE SPONSORS 1992–2002

Continued from previous page

JMK Laing Foundation
Kingsmill Trust
Lady Martin Charity
Leica Ltd
Leicestershire County Council
Loughborough College
Loughborough University
Lyndhurst Charity
Maunsell Structural Plastics Ltd
Moncrieff Charity
Mosaic Dance Group
National Remote Sensing Centre Ltd
New Dulverston Trust
New Durleston Trust
P&O Containers Ltd
Plastech Techtonics Ltd
PLC Communications Ltd
Popeye's Gym
Pultrex Ltd
Rocal Safety Systems Ltd
Royal Hallamshire Hospital Ltd
Saltmine Trust
Starcom Systems (UK) Ltd
Tibetan Foundation
Tigon (UK) Ltd
Tolley Marine Ltd
University of Portsmouth
Virgin Atlantic Airlines
Yang Li Hong

Appendix H

Useful Web Links and Professional Addresses

Paul Lund – Photography   Martin Skinner – Photography
Mike Pritchard – TV and Video   Keith Hopper – TV and Video
John Whatmore – TV and Video   Peter Coulson – TV and Video
Jeremy Brown – Photography   Richard Barlow – Photography

For the professional services, or interest in the work, of the above personnel (or any other PD team member in Appendix F)
please email enquiries for forwarding via: glyn@projectdengke.com or glyndwr@ntlworld.com or glyn@parklandschurch.freeserve.co.uk

For commercial links with China: email CTA_LTD@compuserve.com

How to donate to work of Project Dengke:
http://www.charitynet.org/–care+share/how–to–give.htm
glyn@projectdengke.com

How to get information and/or join prayer list:
Email: glyn@projectdengke.com or glyndwr@ntlworld.com or glyn@parklandschurch.freeserve.co.uk or mel@projectdengke.com or melrichardsonmbe@aol.com

Telephone: 01792 538396 or 01792 589062
or 023 9251 3184 or 023 9284 2322

Project Dengke Friendship Centre:
http://www.projectdengke.com

The Care and Share Foundation:
http://www.charitynet.org/–care+share/

Jian Hua Foundation:
http://www.jhf–hk.org/main.html

Kanding Love Song:
http://members.lycos.co.uk/johnfstudley/Kanding.htm

**Notes on Bengda, the people, the nature reserve,
eco-tourism & agro-forestry**
http://www.geocities.com/john_f_studley/Bengda/Vignettes.htm

John Studley on Dengke/Bengda/Kham
http://members.lycos.co.uk/johnfstudley [click on papers]

Kham Bibliography & Resources
http://members.lycos.co.uk/johnfstudley/khambook.htm

Interactive Map & Photos of Kham & the Hengduan Mountains
http://members.lycos.co.uk/johnfstudley/
interactive_map_of_hengduan_moun.htm

Black Panther Tribute Song
http://www.projectdengke.com

Mel Richardson Professional CV
http://www.tech.port.ac.uk/staffweb/richardm/

Appendix I

Dengke (Luoxu)
Acknowledgements and thanks to Ang Luo and John Studley.

Sichuan Province

Sichuan Province is located in central and south west China. Larger than France, it is known to the Chinese as 'the land of heavenly abundance'. If it were a country it would be the 8th largest in the world with a population around 120,000,000. Both Chengdu (6 million) the provincial capital, and Chongqing (14 million) a major city on the River Yangtze, have populations greater than Greater London.

The Sichuan Basin to the east is a rolling, lush, vast, beautiful expanse of fertile land. The main output is grain, cotton, edible oil, silk, tea, sugar, vegetables, tobacco, fruit and medicinal herbs. This is a key element of the overall agricultural policy of the whole of China. Large areas are also given over to palm, rattan, straw and bamboo —the latter being an essential food for one of Sichuan's most famous natives: the giant panda. The numbers of this much-loved, cuddly, wild creature are down to around 1000 and it tends to only inhabit the western edge of Sichuan, close to the Tibetan highlands.

Sichuan is rich in mineral reserves, with deposits of copper, tin, aluminium, zinc, nickel, titanium, coal and mica. In the west there is also said to be lithium and on one coach stop in the mountains on our journey to Dengke we witnessed particles of gold glistening in a mountain stream. Interestingly, the province's water reserves account for a quarter of the nation's total, also providing a significant source of renewable energy for use in industry and agriculture. Huge, £100 bn, investment programmes are planned for the Yangtze Valley.

This region is also one of the most important industrial bases in China. Building on the industrial backbone provided by the cities of Chongqing, Chengdu, Zigong, Neijiang and Dukou, the province now has over 400 principal enterprises and tens of thousands of smaller ones. Sichuan is sub-divided into a number of prefectures, of which Ganzi is one of the most westerly.

Ganzi Autonomous Tibetan Prefecture.

Ganzi Prefecture covers an area of 150,000 km² (27% of the area of Sichuan Province) and has its capital at Kangding. It has 1.4 million Mu of pastoral grassland (15 Mu = 1 Hectare) and 27.1% of the total area is given over to forestry. 75.5% of the total population of 830,000 are Tibetan and there are 21 ethnic groups. There are 18 counties covering 326 townships, at an average altitude of 3,500m. Local officials claim that there is an untapped hydroelectric potential of over 37 million kW. Natural resources are clearly in abundance including minerals, ferrous metals, non-ferrous metals, gold, copper, bronze, silver, and herbs. The 5 million estimated livestock include yak, horses, pigs, goats, and sheep. In terms of medical practice, the prefecture has 4,100 doctors (30% Tibetan) and 320 hospitals and units. 120 doctors work in provincial government hospitals, and 280 in local private hospitals. Each county has a hospital, a vaccination clinic, and a mother and child unit. 79 of the districts in the prefecture have their own hospital and there are 222 hospitals amongst the 326 townships. Although one third of all townships do not have a hospital, the current five year plan seeks to correct the imbalance. 7 out of the 18 counties have a specifically Tibetan hospital (averaging 7 staff) with the largest located at Kangding. Kangding has 50 beds served by 40 doctors and nurses, and Dege 20 beds served by 20 staff. Also there is a medical training school at Kangding with three Tibetan classes, 4 years training, and three courses to associate professor level. Ten students have graduated and been placed in local hospitals. Interestingly, it is quite rare for people to stay overnight in hospital. Dege (not far from Dengke down the Yangtze River) is the cultural centre for Tibetan medicine. It has its own pharmaceutical factory for making medicines —for arthritis, and for nervous and stomach problems.

Dengke Village

The statistics associated with Dengke are quite interesting. The name itself means 'Deng's valley', commemorating the warrior who was given the area in the spoils of battle. Some say a township has been on the site for over 2000 years. In essence, Dengke is a 3000-person village, in Luoxu Township, in Shiqu County, in Ganzi Autonomous Tibetan Prefecture, in Sichuan Province, in the Peoples Republic of China. (See photograph and figure in illustrated section.) It is at an altitude of 3,500m, in a valley setting, in a mainly agricultural area (green barley, wheat, peas, cabbage, tomatoes etc). The main livestock, which sometimes seem to wander around loose, are yak, cows, goats, and sheep.

Prior to our 1992 expedition we were told by public health officials that Dengke had the largest hospital in the group of four villages that made up the township of Luoxu. It had over 10 doctors and nurses, though the Tibetan doctor had recently moved on. Care had to be taken with animal husbandry due to the possibility of diseases such as "Bao Luan Chong Bin", and stomach disease. Leprosy patients were isolated as a matter of policy. An interesting mix of Tibetan/Chinese/Western medicine was practised in the hospital, and our own doctors came to have a great regard for the skills and expertise of the local practitioners (who had to go about their work with very little, or no, equipment and drugs).

Primary schooling was found to start at seven years old. There are big cultural problems with itinerants and nomadic peoples, however, and it is not unusual to find that schooling does not start until 11/12 years (if at all). Junior High School is for 13–16 year olds, and this is attained by only 10% of Primary School children. Senior High School is for 16–19 year olds (outside Dengke) and this is only attained by 3% of Junior High School children. Education beyond 19 years is effectively non-existent. The authorities and teachers seem very mindful of the problems and are working hard to improve matters e.g. boarding school education is on offer to nomadic groups (who move four times a year) but the offer is rarely taken up. The Tibetan dialect of Kangba is spoken in the Dengke Region and also Ando in the outer Agricultural and Pastoral Regions. Both dialects are used at all levels of schooling, although Mandarin predominates in class. Tibetan as a subject is also available.

The Environment of Dengke

Dengke (Luoxu Township) is located at the east bank of the upper reaches of the Golden Sand River (the River Yangtze). It is at the junction of Sichuan Province, Qinghai Province and Xizang Autonomous District (Tibetan). To the west is Jiangda county of Xizang Autonomous District on the other side of the Golden Sand River, and is bounded on the north by Yushu Prefecture in Qinghai Province. Compared with the surrounding highly elevated areas, the natural conditions in Dengke are good. There is 68,900 mu of cultivable land, 93,500 mu of forest area and 3,198,100 mu of grassland (1 mu = 0.0667 ha or hectares. 1 ha = 2.5 acres = 10,000m²). The drainage area of the Golden Sand River and its main tributaries reaches over 2,390 square kilometres. The altitude drops of the Golden Sand River and its main tributaries are over 280m and 1,000 m respectively. The theoretical reserves of hydraulic energy are estimated at over 260,000 kW. Rainfall is abundant, with average annual precipitation reaching over 569 mm. It is rich in solar energy resources, with annual sunshine time >2,000–2,500 hours, and the annual radiation >130–160 kilo calories/cm² (1 Joule = 0.25 calories). Compare this to the annual solar energy received across the United States, which ranges from lows of about 300 calories/cm²/yr to 500+ calories/cm²/yr. The annual average temperature is 5.7 °C, and the temperature difference between day and night can be as high as 40 degC.

Luoxu Town is quite rich in mineral resources. Among the proven deposits worth mining, there are the tin ore in Luoxu, the manganese mine in the area of Zhenda, the goldmine near Zhengke. Superior mineral resources will no doubt play an important role in the development of Luoxu.

There are many rare wild animals living in Luoxu, six types having been listed by the State as requiring government protection, as have four types of bird. Among these, the wild yak, white-lipped deer, argali, black neck crane, and the golden vulture are especially famous. Golden eagles and various types of kite are increasingly found on the surrounding grasslands.

Luoxu teems with rare medicinal herbs and animal products, such as Chinese caterpillar fungus (cordyceps sinensis), the bulb of fritillary (fritillaria thunbergii), the fruit of Chinese wolfberry (lycium chinense), Hongjintian, Chinese rhubarb, bezoar, pilose antler (of a young stag), musk, leopard bone, bear gallbladder etc., although the latter are now banned.

Further references to Dengke and its history may be found on the following website: http://members.lycos.co.uk/johnfstudley [click on papers]